Introduction

Cara Watson's winning poetry has an simplicity that belies the depth of the subject. In 'Photo' little is directly expressed to elegantly evoke a rich image, 'He stares from the edge,/ frayed in his suit and/ dead carnation.' And in 'Asylum Seeker' the phrasing of a single simile commands more attention than many complete poems achieve, 'He spits/words/ like lemon pips[...]'

It is good to have editing assumptions challenged, as the winning story *In Terra Pax* did for my typographical dislike for block capitals; here Paul Brownsey makes amusing use of the convention and I could find no better substitute. The narrative calls for frequent and marked volume; a melodrama that plays on cultural tensions and awkwardness in a hospital setting. A locale shared by Lucy Durneen's darker 'Everything Beautiful is Far Away', which likewise draws on circumstance to address anxieties and expectations.

Perspective, as Durneen's title hints, plays an important role. And no less so in the magical realist 'With New Eyes' by Janet Holst, which recalls the whimsy of Gogol or Kafka or, from amongst the poetry, in Elizabeth Briggs homage to surrealist painter René Magritte's *The Empty Mask* titled 'Behind the Screen', 'and segments of Screen/ laugh as they hide the true picture.'

Rowan B. Fortune
Tŷ Meirion, December 2011

Contents

In Terra Pax
& other stories & poems

Rowan B Fortune
(editor)

Published by Cinnamon Press
Meirion House
Glan yr afon
Tanygrisiau
Blaenau Ffestiniog
Gwynedd LL41 3SU
www.cinnamonpress.com

ISBN 978-1-907090-56-1
British Library Cataloguing in Publication Data. A CIP record for this book can be obtained from the British Library

Designed and typeset in Palatino and Garamond by Cinnamon Press.
Cover design by Jan Fortune-Wood from original artwork 'Hospital' © Hongqu Zhang agency dreamtime.

Cinnamon Press is represented by Inpress and by the Welsh Books Council in Wales.

Printed in Poland

Contributors

In Terra Pax

Jane McLaughlin

Walking Home

He knows the sky. Some days his head
between two cars. Others, butted to the wall,
smell of dog-piss, grit on his lips.
He knows the lightness of white clouds
and the lowering of winter greys.

It doesn't matter which way he takes.
The faces close. The teeth. No eye contact.
Spaz. Gay. And then the kick
catching the base of his rucksack.
They know better than to mark.

The sky. His bag over the fence.
The faces above him. circling, sliding.
His coat in a puddle, trainers flung two ways,
chest squeezed like bellows
under a classmate's foot.

He knows the wind. He feels it on his face
as quietness rests again on the stones.
It cools his face, says go home now.
He has to move the way clouds do,
slipping silently along.

He knows the sky
from which there is no escape
and the blowing of the wind
that tells him he's alone.
If he gets home with both shoes
it is enough.

Two Scoops

Artist of *les glaces*, his palette shines
in stainless steel trays. Blueberry, crimson,
shades of banana, peach and coffee.
The slopes of brilliant glaciers invite,
dug out by silver hemispheres.

Gourmet flavours: *fraise et basilic,*
sorbet de melon, poire et cannelle.
Deux boules. Two scoops, four dollars fifty.
He places each on the balanced cornet.
pressing gently so the edge furls.

In my hand, now, here in Quebec, midsummer.
And I'm back on the sands at Caswell
with the prize of the afternoon:
A latticed cornet printed 'Askeys'
and crowned with two glistening scoops.

The long wait past lunchtime, and the walk at last
to the beach kiosk. A cornet in the hand.
Most days just vanilla, strawberry. Sometimes
the rare green of pistachio, exotic stripes
of neapolitan, caverns of chocolate.

A lick, a crunch, gone like cerise bubbles
of cherryade, or hot sugar miraculously
spinning into clouds. Vanished too soon
whether dripping pinkly in Gower sun
or going squashy in Mumbles rain.

Guruji

You sent me home,
  an orange begonia in my pocket
and Sanskrit in my ears.

At the bus stop I grip your absurd flower
  and think how you always drive sense to its limit.

For three days it smoulders in my kitchen
  at the bottom of the frosted vase.

Your voice clangs like a great gong:
  'Say it in Latin!' and I do,
and the Sanskrit chimes back at me
  sometimes so close that I believe
I look into the eyes of a woman speaking
  the ancient Indo-European mother language.

Neighbours say 'Yes, the Hindu lady,
  we can't hear her sing
now she's got her double glazing.'

Your tabla and harmonium
  rest among embroidered cushions.
Buses stop and start with a snarl of gears
  closing your song of evening.

Your puja-room
  tinselled and velvet
with texts you wrote in gold
  saves me more than you know
from a summer that went cold
  and out of tune.

Scylla's Workshop

Today she has them writing about the sea.
They ask about the barking. She says:
It's in their heads: seals far away on ice.
They ask about the fronds trailing from her satchel.
She says it's carrageen for pudding.

Discussion of orcas and narwhals, speculation
on the slow algous coupling of octopi.
Diamond cliffs flecked with petrels rear
at their backs. The songs of whales and silkies
wind in the chambers of their ears.

She explains the grammar of tides and currents,
how charts and sextants did not save
old sailors from the teeth of storms
and those who rode in blue-eyed boats
turned giddy in the pull of siren songs.

They write of the nacre spirals hidden
in the nautilus, the carving of scrimshaw.
They do not notice the water rising steadily
outside the windows, translucent green,
a narrative of silver surface, voracious straits.

Ribbons of kelp brush silky against the glass,
sequinned predators girn their needled jaws.
Too late they feel the water licking at their feet.
As heads of dogs appear around her waist
she breathes the stink of rotten flesh.

Everything Beautiful is Far Away
Lucy Durneen

One night there was a man in the lobby who said he had to come from the Isle of Man to visit his wife; this was the only hospital that could treat her cancer. The only one? Really? Well no, there were others, he said. But here they could do things that would give her months and not weeks. Wasn't that worth the trip? I am not the kind of person to answer strangers. But I mean, I didn't know.

We watched the revolving doors instead of talking to each other, wondering who had it worst; the doctors who knew everything, going outside for a smoke, or the mothers who knew nothing, stubbing their cigarettes out on the wall as they ran in. I wondered this. The man in the lobby was probably thinking of other things. If I had to guess, if I was made to, I would say that weeks might be better, but that is because I am an impatient kind of person. You go through life wanting time to speed up so you can be old enough to drive, or spend a hundred quid on a pair of shoes without asking your mother's permission. You just want someone to take you seriously. You don't want anything to be measured in periods longer than weeks.

They say that actually mothers always know. It is a vastness of knowledge that means nothing is exempt. It is like taxi drivers who can hold the entire London A-Z in their heads, even long after they have had their licences revoked because their reactions are too slow to be allowed in charge of a car. It kicks in right at the moment of that first beat of the infant heart, as does the sacrifice, the way you never look as good as you did before no matter how much weight you lose. I don't call this suffering myself. I say, you make your bed. What I'm really saying is that I could never be a doctor. There might be miracles but you still have the feeling they are bracing themselves for something else. That thing is afterwards. It's the thing nobody ever speaks of.

I watched the revolving doors like they were in a film, like this was the OK Corral and any minute now we were going to have to dodge the spray of fire. I was just about ready to duck when the man in the lobby said; I have to go up and give her a sponge bath now. They want me to have an active role in her care. Do they make you do that?

They don't. I have made it quite clear from the start what I am and am not prepared to do.

Outside the hospital there are fields, wheat I think because historically this is bread-making country. You still see windmills when you drive out over the fen, but they don't work except on public holidays, when people come from all over to make bread as a way of bringing the past to life.

You can see the fields from any of the windows, if you look, but that is not why the windows in hospitals are there. It is not about the view. If you have ever lived by the sea you will know this. The wildness—it doesn't go away when you can't see it. I thought about the woman from the Isle of Man, how when she closed her eyes she could have the whole ocean if she wanted, like a long, living dream.

There is a name for the way you might want to stay in the dream and not come back. Cousteau called it rapture of the deep, but he was talking the state of nitrous intoxication experienced by divers, an entirely reversible condition as long as you know to ascend to the shallows. It is not a sickness so much as not realising when you have had too much.

At night you can hear the wheat, like a song, like the sea. You hear the hum of ancient glacial planes beneath long barrows.

Suddenly the surface seems very far away.

At five o'clock a nurse comes to give him morphine. You can have it through a pump or in a kind of lollipop like you are five years old, except two people have to sign it off from the pharmacy. There is one nurse; she talks to him like I never have. She touches him in a way that should make me jealous. That blue diamond inside the wrist. Poor love, she says, rubbing it afterwards. Poor baby.

You notice this too when people speak to small children, or animals, how they change the tone of their voice, or make incomprehensible hand gestures. Before there was language, people communicated with their hands. And yet, when there are

14

no words, we forget there was a time when it was okay to tell people how we feel.

My sister used to say, when she was la-ing nursery rhymes late into the night with Anna, well it can only ever help to try. It would take so long some nights, my sister putting Anna in the rugby ball position and swaying from side to side saying, *there there baby, la la,* a thousand times. At the worst of it I might think, *for the love of God Anna!* or I might come in and take over, it depended on how things were with my sister, if I felt sorry for her or if she had brought up the thing about the money I borrowed from our parents. But if I did go in, there was something I knew for certain, which was that Anna would stop crying. She'd just stop and the triumph would be mine, which you would think I would feel good about. But all it did was make my sister feel as though she had failed in the most basic biological way. My sister would have preferred the crying to that. So on the nights I felt sorry for her, what I did was put the pillow over my head and go back to sleep.

I wanted to say to the man in the lobby, let the nurses do the sponge bath: let it go. Only my sister would know how this feels.

To start with you talk about everything. Arguments are not off limits either. Then there are the things which ordinarily wouldn't be funny enough to mention, but it turns out not so many things happen in a day, or even a week; you can't be picky. I ask him if he remembers when we went to Starcross. We drove all the way along the coast of what they call the English Riviera, where palm trees grow next to signs for fish and chips. You know, I say, I wore that patchwork skirt. You hated it because it made me look like a hippy. There were owls flying over the beach even though it was daylight. There was this sign, on the wall of the harbour; Shellfish eaten from these waters must be boiled continuously for three minutes. I talk fast. I talk like there is a stopwatch running and any minute someone is going to shout Stop!

His eyes are slow to open so there is time. I think of stone rubbing the back of my knees, the bright bliss of clouds: you remember things like this at the oddest times. My hands like flat stones, splayed out behind me, the weight of the sun, which is the weight of a universe. I was a hippy back then, it's true, my hat had

15

a sunflower stitched to the brim and I even braided my hair. I say I braided it; my sister did it for me each morning. When we went to Starcross I had to leave the braids in, night after night, until the elastic bands became part of my hair, and then my hair became elastic. I could actually stretch it right round the back of my head and still suck on the end of it. But I cut it the next year. That was the last summer I had long hair.

He nods at me, yes, sure I remember. But, he says, an owl flying in the day is not particularly unusual. Later I realise he doesn't remember at all. He can't, because he was not the one who took me to Starcross; it was another man I loved. The guilt rushes through me like my heart is a barrage, just trembling to let go. But I hold it back. I feel it, everything, all of it, like a giant lake, like the Nile behind my heart, dammed.

I read him poetry, sometimes. Mostly I read to him from my magazines. I tell him about the rugby player who has just come out of the closet.

Who knew? It's of no consequence. Let him fuck whom he wants, he says.

Who he wants, I say. Who.

But suddenly I am not sure of anything at all, even grammar.

Across town from the hospital is a hotel building made entirely of glass. This is where I go when it is time to leave the ward. I tell him I am going and he raises a hand in a slow salute. Even at the last minute I turn. Like Orpheus, like Lot's wife, like every TV movie ever made. If I were in a TV movie I would say his name as a question when I turned. And then I would say, quietly; 'Nothing.'

It takes forty five minutes to walk through the city. You could do it in a cab in less than ten, but if you have never run away from anything then you will not know what it is to need the power of your own limbs.

The city at night is submarine, dark, like a Caspar David Friedrich. I paddle downstream. I slip in and out of streets like they are bays and I am a boat, nudging into harbour. Any floating vessel will do; the Jumblies went to sea in a sieve. I cast out and

16

sail into the centre of the moonlit city and I wear the silence like a fur. All about my feet I see the stars and I am treading on the stars. With just my feet I kick whole constellations into touch.

The foyer is like any regular hotel foyer except you can look out of every wall and anyone can look in. Anyone can see me; even the darkness is transparent. I think, this is what the sharks must see in the aquarium. I move through corridors into other worlds, silent as a shark.

If I stay the night depends on two things: whether or not I am angry and whether or not he is angry. There are subtler ways of communicating anger than I ever knew.

Perhaps I will not forgive him for the owls.

Underneath this other man I at least have the decency not to move. His weight like water. My blood like a foreign tide.

Now whenever I am in a tall building the urge to jump is reverent.

They don't provide meals for visitors, even regular ones, but we have struck a deal with the Thai orderly who brings the food. He is fed through a naso-gastric tube, but we fill in a menu for him anyway and the Thai orderly says nothing as long as I give him last week's *Hello* magazine and rub his arse as he leaves. Not everyone thinks hospital food is worth this kind of subterfuge but I was a child of the Eighties. If it didn't come out of a box, a packet or a boilable plastic bag I didn't eat.

The coffee is terrible though.

In the cafeteria I see the man from the lobby, which gives me the sudden urge to buy him a latte. Maybe it is just because he is familiar and all. It is late, but I think I might want to tell him something. His eyes seem far away. He says, Damn fine coffee, to which I answer, And hot! which shows both our age and a mutual preference for surreal and morally questionable drama.

Someone has left a newspaper on the table, open at a page that chronicles the history of the search for extra-terrestrial life. We haven't got very far in fifty years, it turns out. The Filipino waitress shouts, Closing! and the noise of the security grille descending drowns out the section I start to read aloud.

Do you think, the man from the lobby says later, it would be worse if it turned out we are alone in the universe after all?

*

We went to marriage counselling a few times, which some people find surprising and to this I say: illness doesn't make you a saint. Anger is the real problem for us both. The counsellor says that very often it is not the loss of an actual thing that makes us angry, but all the potential things. This was a long time ago and it was in response to his complaint that I never do the washing up, which we learned—I learned—is not about good domestic hygiene but respect. When you are fighting over the dirty coffee cups you are really saying, *love me*. But now I understand what it is the counsellor actually meant.

It becomes very important to have tried scuba diving. It becomes important to have eaten shellfish that have not been boiled continuously for at least three minutes, or to fuck *whom* you want. Knowledge becomes the important thing. I have never been to the circus so I cannot say for sure that it is exploitative of animals. I have so little right to take part in so many debates.

It becomes very important to have been in love, truly in love, the kind that crosses continents and survives the darkest parts of history.

This is something I would show you if I could. I should explain that there is a stone plaque above the reception desk in the hospital lobby, carved to look as if it is really old. But you can tell it isn't because of the shape of the letter 's'. The plaque says *Whatever it is, it will pass*. And what you think is, yes—but when?

There is a woman in this city whose name I will never know so I imagine her as Bella, which was the name of my first dog. The woman might not even be from the city. People come to this hospital from all over the world. Our eyes meet in the mirror of the bathroom in nuclear medicine. You too? she says.

I say nothing. I am dispensing soap. I don't even know what she means. Me? Then I understand yes, she means me, there is no-one else here. I run my hands over the warm tap to rinse them, but it feels good so I hold them there another minute. The water starts to steam and hurt but I don't take my hands away. I know her look; I have worn it myself. I want to say it is hopeful, but the word I really want is famished.

It will pass, she says.

The sting of my hands? No.

What if it doesn't? I ask, and I can see she has never thought of that. My mother used to say I had a cruel streak, but I always thought that was her own cruel streak giving vent, like a volcanic fissure that erupts where it finds fellow igneous rock.

In the mirror my shape is feral. I have crow's feet. I look out of them but they are not my eyes. I look up and what I see is not the ceiling but a closed lid. They say fluorescent light is the most unflattering kind, but in it what I feel is savage and not myself. This is just flattery in disguise. What else is flattery but telling you that you look like something you are not, to make you feel better about the thing that you are.

The hospital soap is called Hibiscrub, which might refer to inhibiting bacteria, but the overwhelming perfume says to me, *hibiscus*. A delicacy in Mexico; the national flower of Malaysia. Tahitian women wear a single red hibiscus behind their ear to show they are ready to be a wife. In the mirror crimson petals bloom violently against my cheek. The last thing I want to smell of is flowers. I run my hands under the tap, rubbing hard on the back and front the way the surgeons do. I hook right in under the nails. The door bangs shut behind the woman I call Bella, but I do not stop scrubbing. I might have been doing it for half an hour; it might be I am there all day. This is what I want to show you: it doesn't pass.

One night I tell the nurses I won't be there in the morning. He raises his hand as I go. He says, pass me the mirror, I want to do my hair. Then he says, I liked it when you were a hippy. I say, you didn't know me when I was a hippy. But then I turn. I say his name, like a question.

I sit in the patients' lounge, in the dark. I pull the vertical blinds and listen to the winter wind, coming in from far away. It has never frightened me like it does some people. I try to imagine what it is to be far away and realise this; that I am too close.

19

What I realise is that everything beautiful is far away.

I haven't been to the glass hotel in two nights. I catch the bus home and then I take the car that has been sitting in the garage these past seven months and drive half way across the country to Starcross. Around Birmingham I realise I have left my mobile in his bedside locker, along with the book I am reading and my hairbrush.

I start to think in threes, as if what I can see in front of me is not the slope of the motorway, but just the beginning, the middle and an end.

There is no colour along the coast apart from the sea pinks, brave in what is still moonlight. Winds hit heavy against the groynes. The air that blows in through my window smells of gulls and tanker oil and the radio plays a cover version of The Smiths song, *Please Please Please let me get what I want*. The piano rises and I listen, and what I think is: how can you get what you want if you don't know what that is?

By morning the sky and the waves are the same, smashing down against the sand which looks like snow, which all along the edge of the world is as fine as snow.

I lied about what I said when I left his room. But I cannot repeat it again, the words I used.

The other man I loved had black hair, like a Romany. Who am I to presume that *he* loved? I think of that song, Scarborough Fair and I wonder if he remembers me at all. Last night I couldn't remember to pick up my mobile phone and suddenly all my memories are being dredged in long draughts, from somewhere old, as if the seventy eight per cent of my body that is water is being restored to clouds, or waves. As if I am returning to the sea.

A gull flies out of the surf and alights on the sand, then another. But it is in fact the same bird. In flight; in suspension above the swell. When I reach Starcross the shellfish sign is still there on the harbour wall and it's been fifteen years.

Even at this hour there is a man selling chips from a truck stand. I am like one of those crazy people who will talk to anyone. I tell the vendor about the gay rugby player. Last week's news, he says. He tugs at a Chelsea scarf and says, Do I look like a man who cares?

On the other side of the wall the water shudders in, the visible surface tremor of an innately rocking world. A bottle slaps the stone, eddies down and goes under. Today the sea is a breathing sheet of lead. The entire sea is a stone, shattering. I am out of metaphors. The sea is just the sea. This is the Earth. In space we are just the remnants of ancient, accidental collisions. But this doesn't explain our longing, or desire. It is obscene, if you think about it, the way we take so long to realise anything.

Here is one way to look at it. It is like the shock of realising that nothing is new, that you—still so resiliently unclonable—are not new. I don't mean this in any zen kind of way, I mean it the way it sounds. Sometimes you can think that you were the one to discover something only to find out that everybody knew about it all along. It is always a shock to learn that other people have been in the same place as you. Even America was there before Columbus.

There is a pencil on my desk that says 'I used to be a Paper cup!' in black stencilled letters down the side. I know this is possible, that we can recycle anything, but still I find myself holding my pencil in wonder and crying.

When people ask I will say it was peaceful. But I won't know. How can any of us know this?

I eat my chips. I wave down to the beach as if there is somebody out there who will realise it is me. I call a name, just to hear it aloud, just to allow it to enter, for a moment, a different world.

Not the past, not the future. Not paradise not reality not a dream.

It is only last week I read him that poem.

Last week's news.

Here is something else I do not know. If it passes—what then?

Elizabeth Briggs

Another Ophelia

The mad scene is about to ensue. A black girl enters
stage left, cradling an empty soup pan,
soothing its curves with nursery rhymes.

Her cries soar beyond the balconies,
aiming to pierce hearts, but it falls
like dead sycamore seeds, never to birth new trees.

Her song promises a storm of heart-break,
which crashes on deaf hearts, the family audience wriggle
deeper into red buffed chairs, programmes fanning their brows.

It is the hero's 'to be or not to be' they revere
the soldier's courtier's eye, the providence of a sparrow,

not the unseen threads the girl weaves,
her spider-legs buckling under a wave of grief,
which *seems* to rock the body deep.

Another Ophelia is doomed to sleep.

Time is softer

you don't have to race the poison
or sweet-tongue the nectar

it is not life or death every second
it is not heaven or hell every second

there's a quiet between each tick
which expands with every in-breath

it's in this timeless quiet of expansion
between the strings of harps and guitars

between the drum beats of Africa
and the salsa steps of Spain

there's a softness you remember
of mother-hush, a deepening lullaby shush

in the dreams carried by feather-breath songs
in the petals of unfurling roses

and the indent your head leaves on your pillow
and rises again, like the sun

Behind the Screen
Inspired by Magritte's The Empty Mask

Ghosts glare at you from a Doily Sky as
you scratch your back on Steel-Wood knobs but
whilst you are framing Screen, your dreams
ignite House with no matches.
Sky kidnaps House into irregular shapes
as Doilies suffocate Fire, though Wood
promised not to burn and scar
Tablecloth, but House is already running
from Steel Sky, and segments of Screen
laugh as they hide the true picture.

Ian McEwen

Shadows

What busy lives the shadows lead.
They are limber enough

for anything, flat out on the grass,
or climbing the walls.

They keep up full pelt
with the train. They read

all the textures of the earth
the way cheese reads the grater.

They go to bed at night.
Who gets up in the morning?

Aphrodite, restored

She has learned all she needs
to about fashions,
they navigate the rings
of gravel in degrees
of heaviness, as planets.

She has learned all she needs
to about the deft
wind, how it molests
the plants that never
wake.

The sun beats around
like a trapped bird
and the stupid moon
the same but quieter
and much less yellow.

A dizziness of pushchairs.
The flicker of gardeners
and the colours snap
forth and back.

She has learned all she needs
to about rain
and the fog also.

One day she wants to work
with children one day she wants
to know what 'naked' means.

Poem with woman

The unassumed parade
wardrobe to wash-box
across the lucid staves
of half-drawn curtains.

How fold and fallows
haul and skein,
the cream and supple moulds
of flesh imagine

out the morning. Our
old glass is a kind
of stretch-mark over
light, that otherwise

never might know
itself: inflection
all there is to show
by way of sign,

to taste the hour lapse
or work our history,
fallow, fold, cream, or trap
that beauty

falling to it.

Rosie Garland

Laying fire

The doctor, with a name-tag I can't recall
by the time you've driven me home,
tells me that chemotherapy affects the memory.
Another nail knocked into the fence of side-effects hemming me in.

We rent a cottage for the weekend, before I'm too sick
to get away from all of it. For the first time
in twenty years I squat before the dead heap
of last night's fire; scrape out ash,
twist newspaper, the dried-out peel of oranges,
a crumbled firelighter, knit kindling into a tent of split pine.

It catches first time. My knuckles are black with soot.
Before I can eat, I take a nail-brush and scrub until pink, raw.

I have this dance

February evening: grappling
the foot of the bed for balance, unpeeling
first one sock then the other, aching
to lie down, for fadeout, for the horizontal plane of the bed;

you come in to the room. Press your mouth
to the warm exhaustion of my scalp, rest there;
arms circling me into the skip of your heart,
and take my hand in an unvoiced *may I have this dance?*

Sway a slow waltz, three lengthening steps,
three more; turn me away
for one long breath, then pull me back.
I have a then and now. I have this dance.

Hosanna in Mare Street
Eithne Nightingale

I love St Augustine's churchyard. The squirrels scampering up the sycamore trees: the lone sixteenth century church tower bereft of its nave and chapels long since demolished. It has been tided up and is better lit than it used to be. The heroine needles have been swept away and, at night, I no longer fear that addicts will jump out from behind the graves. The churchyard has become a sanctuary. A place where couples, friends and families sit and talk and people walk their dogs. It provides a moment's respite between my terraced Victorian house in a quiet cul-de-sac and the madness of the high street. I know what awaits me. The unruly bus queues outside the betting shop: people selling the Big Issue or urging me to sign a petition. But for the moment I want to enjoy the wind tussling the leaves, the scent of roses teasing my nostrils and the sound of the bells from the eighteenth century church nearby. I could be in any English village.

'Nice legs,' slurs a white middle-aged man lounging on a bench with crushed cans of Red Stripe at his feet.

'Yes, nice legs ' repeats his friend with a Polish accent, raising his beer can in salute.

I ignore them. Best not to engage.

An African woman pushes a ladybird buggy with a red parasol covered in large black spots towards me. The woman looks magnificent in a swirling headdress and matching purple and green suit with puff sleeves and a hip hugging skirt that flares out from her knees. Her daughter, with hair in tight bunches that spring from her head, snuggles into her ladybird buggy and chews her toy tiger.

A bike whizzes past at enormous speed causing the mother to swerve. The tiger is thrown from the buggy and the child starts to howl.

'Look out,' cries the woman. 'You nearly killed my daughter.' The cyclist takes no notice and is gone. I rescue the tiger.

'Say thank you,' instructs the mother, but the child will not accept her tiger from a stranger so throws it out again.

'Wicked child,' cries the mother as she picks up the tiger and lays it on the buggy handlebars. The tiger goes limp as if worn out by the drama.

'Nice bum,' says the middle-aged man as the African woman passes by.

She turns and lets out a string of abuse in some unknown language. I admire this woman—the way she pushes the ladybird buggy as if it were a sedan chair carrying an empress, the parasol protecting her daughter from the mid-day sun.

As I approach the lone church tower, I hear a young man bellowing into a microphone. He is young and black and surrounded by a group of girls, also black, who cheer him on, clapping their hands. They are Jehovah's Witnesses, no doubt, who often knock on my door at the most inconvenient time. I do my best to avoid them, peeping through the living room curtains and not answering the door. But this time they are standing in my path.

'Sing hosanna,' cries the young man, tapping his trainers in time to the beat.

'Sing hosanna,' echo the girl chorus, banging their tambourines.

A number 38 trundles down the high street and halts at the bus stop. An Asian man with a trilby hat tries to push through the crowd.

'Don't worry about missing the bus. Worry about missing the rapture,' cries the young preacher.

The Asian man stumbles.

'Oh,' gasp the crowd as if in awe of this young man who appears to have invoked God to prevent the man catching the bus; giving him a chance to find his rapture.

The man uses the upright grave to pull himself up, dusts himself down, retrieves his hat, swears at the young preacher and gets on the bus just as it pulls away. The bus conductor has been waiting for him.

As the bus moves off the young preacher adjusts his baseball cap, turning it back to front and resumes his rousing.

'Young people. You're lucky. You've got time to come back to Jesus. Many people are dead today.'

Two white women, past their prime, drag their identical tartan trolleys down the high street and towards the Pound Shop where the seller of the Big Issue helps them up the steps.

'Older people too. You don't have much time before the fire licks around you. Turn to Jesus before it's too late.'

The women, their faces coated in powder and their hair dyed

31

except for the tell tale roots, mutter under their breath. They seem none too happy to be reminded of their imminent death.

'You can't buy salvation in the Pound Shop. Salvation is free.'

But the women are more concerned about their weekly shop. I am mesmerized, intrigued by the young man's turn of phrase, his uncanny knack of involving us all in his drama. I sit on an upright grave in earshot, but a safe distance away so I am not a target for salvation.

'God ain't a liar.'

'God ain't a liar,' echo the chorus.

'The devil's a liar.'

'The devil's a liar.'

The chorus clap their hands and sway to the rhythm of his words, their words.

'When you get to the doors of hell, God will ask, 'Did you listen to that black boy in Mare Street?' 'No,' you will reply.'

'No,' shout the young girls.

'You can have all the GCSEs in the world and still God won't accept you. I don't have none of that. No maths, no English, no geography, but still God has taken me in.'

'God has taken you in,' cry the chorus.

'I've got the power within me.'

'You've got the power within you.'

The girls' voices get shriller, their look more ecstatic.

A couple of Vietnamese girls in tight white trousers and sling back stilettos join the crowd.

'My church delivers. Not like Buddha. Not like Ying and Yang and all that rubbish. Their gods don't deliver.'

The girls raise their eyebrows, smirk and walk away in the direction of the Vietnamese nail parlour with a smiling Buddha in the window. They have more earthly matters on their mind.

The Red Stripe drinkers have brought their friends to join in the entertainment.

'Hail hosanna,' they sing, swaying towards each other, then back again to right themselves.

'The devil is behind alcohol,' shouts the preacher boy.

'Hail hosanna,' croak the drunks. Some of them even have good voices.

A group of Green Peace activists arrive and set up a stall outside McDonalds. Preacher boy does not want to be upstaged.

'Forget about global warming and all that nonsense. The world is going to end anyway.'

The activists hold up their cardboard placards, 'Cut carbon emissions.'

'I wish the world would end today,' cries the young preacher.

'It will end soon,' shouts a lanky white activist. 'But at the hands of man not God.'

'We don't come from no fish, no monkey,' shouts preacher boy.

'Could have fooled me,' says one of the drunkards.

'God made me.'

'Wish he hadn't bothered,' shouts another.

The preacher is undeterred. God has made him bold.

'How can the world be created with a big bang? If I crash a Mercedes or a BMW into a bus what do I get? '

A skateboard approaches, crashes through the backing group and lands at the feet of the preacher boy.

'See, God has spoken. If that young boy crashes his skateboard, what do you get?'

'An accident,' cry the girl chorus, downing swigs of Pepsi.

The skater, a mixed race boy in tight shorts, stands up and retrieves his skateboard. He whips a Pepsi out of one of the girl's hands and skates off.

'Thieving is sinful. That skater boy will rot in hell.'

'Thieving is sinful,' chant the chorus.

And then the truth comes out, the confessional.

'My name is Andre. I too used to be a thief. I used to rob people in the middle of the night and that's what God does. He comes in the middle of the night.'

A few people raise their eyebrows. Even the drunks have calmed down.

'I used to be a member of a gang and still God has accepted me. He saved me from robbing. He saved me from killing.'

My respect for the work of the black churches rises. Far better to have a mad evangelist preacher than someone who knifes his peers or robs people in the middle of the night.

Four buses come down the high street. Since the days of Ken Livingstone, the last Mayor of London, the high street has been choked with buses.

'If the 254 catches fire and you don't get off, you're stupid. You're going to get burnt.'

Sirens ring and people look round, wary that God may

intervene and the bus will spontaneously explode, such is the terror in the young man's voice.

'Do you want to die for your sins and go to hell? Hell is a real place. Get me.'

The sound of sirens gets closer and three panda cars drive up. Maybe this performance is a cover for a robbery in McDonalds and the preacher boy has not reformed after all.

'I don't care if ten policemen come and get me. I will go to the cells. I will speak.'

And then I see the gold cross around his neck. It looks familiar. Small and delicate decorated with garnets and emeralds. I move forwards. It is unmistakable. Just like the one given to me by my godmother on my confirmation.

The police get out of their car. I recall the day I got back from work, my house ransacked, my belongings scattered down the street. I wait expecting the police to take the young evangelist away. I am tempted to shout out, 'The preacher boy is wearing my cross. He stole it from my house.'

But the police walk past the young evangelist. They are only interested in the Red Stripe drinkers who had admired my legs. The other drunks complain, incensed to see this mishandling of their mates, but are moved on and the police leave. I have missed my chance to turn in my very own thief.

The African woman, pushing her ladybird buggy with the toy tiger still lying limp over the handlebars, comes flying down the high street.

'Andre. Forget your preaching. I need some help with my bags.'

I am stunned. Are they neighbours? Do they attend the same church? Surely the preacher boy can't be the son of this proud, stately African woman. Andre leans down to tickle the little girl who giggles. The evangelist is clearly not a stranger. Andre says goodbye to his backing group and picks up the woman's shopping.

I walk into Marks and Spencer buying the latest Big Issue on my way in. As I push my trolley between the counters picking out the freshest apples, and the softest avocados my Christian upbringing starts to kick in. Perhaps the young boy has reformed. He deserves a second chance. In any case I have already collected the insurance.

When I come out of the shop, Green Peace supporters have disappeared. In their place is a stall selling Islamic literature. No rabble rousing. No percussion. The bearded man in a long white robe and embroidered cap asks, 'Do you have a personal faith?'

'I used to.'

'You still believe in a God I am sure.'

'Forgiveness perhaps. God, no.'

Ben Parker

One Place

Out here the elms echo with the eagle-shout
and sparrow-cry; leaves tune the wind;
the only path is the one your trespass cuts.

Your car is waiting at the forest's edge
with autumn already falling on its roof.
You bag and bury your mud clad-shoes

before rejoining the nightly homeward grind,
just another commuter tuned to a private frequency.
Delay can be explained by deadlines,

accidents, or at a push affairs. Your wife
would sanction a sexual betrayal far sooner
than bless your return to here,

the one place still forbidden to you both.

The Lake

There is a lake that freezes
once only in a lifetime. Too distant
to be seen from shore although
the lake is small and could be shouted over
on a day the wind is right. The centre
holds an island, squat as a bronze boss
on a silver shimmering shield.
It is miles from the nearest village,
shaded from the sun by a neat
half-moon of craggy, treeless mountains
and is a place you would not visit twice.
But come when weather warnings
have cleared the paths of weekend walkers
and all the native birds have passed you
on their journey south and you might find
the water fastened down with ice.
And if you choose to make the walk
don't stop. The surface cracks
and mutters at your back. Speed up,
keep the looming island in your sight,
the freeze will hold you only once.

A Sign

Some saw it first when driving home from work:
side windows atlases of ice, the melt
not yet complete, the gap just big enough.
Others saw it first when waking up:
too large to be the sun though not as bright,
its colour uniform, its surface smooth
as though a perfect sphere were sliced
in space, the background glow escaped.

All stars except our own have ceased to show
and that one we have started to forget.
This new light always breaks between the trees,
always hangs top-right of any scene.
I note today it's grown, our summer's late.
I haven't slept for weeks.

City of Glass

One morning we woke to find the city
composed entirely of glass, prismatic
in the low sun glancing off sharp edges.
Not one object remained that had not bled
its colour into the ground in the night.
From the deep shock-proof shells of offices
to the etched headlines on delicate sheets
of stacked papers, everything was washed clear.
Only the pavements, foundations and roads
kept unaltered their original form,
supporting the city's fragile sculpture.

And, exposed behind glass walls, carefully
closed glass doors, life continues. A woman
cautiously taps a piano's frail keys,
the silica strings resonate, each note
a high-pitched, drawn-out crystalline scream
that quavers, threatens to, but does not break.

Jacqueline Bulman

Casa Borboleta

How sharp is the flick of love
I feel for you? For your fallen walls
and lack of a road but no, not that,
for your bread oven and stone bees,
neglected grapes, none of these, none.
For the spring water tap up a slate path
where water drips, not this.
To describe you, my love for you:
as much a swift drenching
as a downpour of arrows.

Suddenly felt louder to me

She came in and out of the café
three times before sitting down.
Found a place far from the other tables—
the noise in the main room seeming to hurt her face,
and it suddenly felt louder to me.
When I came to take her order
I guessed she wanted me to notice
the book she was reading: *Stranger Music*
by Leonard Cohen: slowly laid it flat
with a crumpled receipt as a bookmark,
looked at the menu with a smile, as if
it was a weird thing.
She couldn't decide what to order so asked me to help,
but I couldn't, sure I couldn't decide.
She changed her mind twice then settled for
roasted chicken and tomato, got back to her book,
her eyes looking up only once more, when I didn't leave.

With New Eyes
Janet Holst

Gloria Chapstick wasn't a famous writer; she wasn't beautiful or even young anymore, but she aspired, living in hope on the edge of the city in an apartment high above the harbour. The house was shabby, an ill-painted post-war wooden villa down too many steep steps from the road; it shook and creaked in the wind, leaked and sagged, but had glorious views of bush and sea. From her writing desk in her small bedroom she could watch the ferries below scuttling across the harbour, and brightly coloured yachts bending keenly, their sails swollen in the stiff, southerly breezes. She sat staring at this view now, and at the clouds bunching above the green hills opposite. Her mind was grappling with the edge of an idea for her novel, *Nothing Ventured*. Four months ago it had seemed a perfect project. Set in fifth century Rome, it chronicled the fortunes of chaste Pulcheria, who gradually assumes power over her dull, weak brother, only to succumb to charms of...

But in recent weeks the winds of inspiration had slackened, and her craft, off-course, had stalled and beached: now she would have to abandon it. It wasn't her first novel; she'd sold two to a publisher of historical romances. The early one, a tale set in Egypt and told by one of Cleopatra's maids, had done well, encouraging her to think she had struck a seam, one that could lead to a whole series and its attendant book tours, signings with free wine and the steady deposit of royalties in an overseas bank account.

'You just need a holiday,' her old friend Bettina advised her over the phone. 'You need to go somewhere to stir up your creative juices again. What about a trip to Greece? Or Morocco? Somewhere exotic.'

Bettina had a point, but also a dependable income—four hundred sterling a month left by an unknown great uncle in England. Gloria lived tenuously on the cusp of poverty, eking out her writing life by editing an electricians' quarterly, the miserly *Live Wire*. Aside from two trips South each year to stay with her sister, her getaways were more modest: cheap Tuesdays at the local cinema, a ferry ride around the bays and occasional afternoons at a gallery. Even these were barely manageable. No, she would have to devise some other refreshment if she were to salvage the wreck of her writing. Her eyes slid around the room, looking for inspiration.

She liked her small room for its irregularity. It felt like a wheelhouse tilting above the harbour and over the years she had added her own touches: a collection of framed early maps of the Aegean on the walls; an Indian blue cotton spread patterned with green dolphins draping her narrow bed; a large Egyptian blue porcelain cat on the uneven floor by the door and a line of blue African violets along the windowsill. Her desk was old, salvaged from a garage sale; worn manila folders containing her research notes and a thumbed copy of *OED* leaned against her old computer and taped across the top of its screen was the stern reminder, 'Never a day without a line.'

As she gazed across the harbour, the black cat, Oedipus, sprang up on her lap and began a painful, rhythmic kneading of her right thigh. She pushed him away and turned back to her screen, where, in her daydreaming, slow-moving aquatic life had replaced her text. The cat leaped again, hitting the keyboard, scattering the fish and leaving a miscellany of invading letters on her novel script 'gvrfjio]isal.juy   gdsno[mkdssssssso0kv cxkm' ffffffffffffddddddddddddd .' She shoved him off, he squealed and her glasses were ripped from her face, falling with a clatter to the floor, the neck cord was caught in his paw and snapped. She picked them up; they had broken across the bridge. She tried fitting the bits together, thinking to glue them, but the tortoiseshell frame had warped. They had sloped across her face in a rakish way of late, and now she could see another warning fault line etched along the left stem. She'd have to get a new pair. It was something she hated: trying on new shapes, crouched and peering myopically at her face in strangely angled frames under the critical gaze of some smart, unsympathetic sales assistant.

'They can be quite expensive, now,' Bet warned her over the phone. 'You can easily spend $800, or more, for a pair.'

'Well, I don't have that kind of money; the car needs a new clutch.'

'What about second-hand ones? You could try the Op Shop, or Vincent de Paul. They don't throw out things like spectacles. You might just be lucky—and you could get the lenses changed.'

She found a park around the corner from the shop. It was mid-morning. The shoppers were out, but too early for the office

43

lunchtime crowd. Passing an optician's, she glanced in. This year, the frames were narrow, squinting oblongs, a change from last year's rimless kind and the schoolboy rounds before that. Did people really follow such trends? She slipped inside the shop to finger a few price tags. They were coded, unreadable.

'How much are these?' She pointed to a cheeky red frame, hexagonal in shape.

The sales girl studied the label, rolling her tongue in her mouth as she did.

'Would you be having lenses?' she asked, flicking her eyes over Gloria's old gabardine raincoat. 'Or just taking the frames?'

'Why?'

'Excuse me?'

'Why would the price be different if I bought lenses as well?'

The girl blinked, challenged. 'It's our policy.' She paused. 'These are $399, but with lenses there'd be a discount.'

'I'll think about it,' said Gloria, and headed for the door.

Two doors down the Op Shop was empty, except for a girl reading at the counter. Gloria wandered along a row of camphoric women's jackets and skirts. Turning at the end of the aisle, she bumped against a woman browsing among the men's jackets and trousers and then saw, on a shelf in the corner, a tangle of large spectacles. She reached for the smallest pair, a bright green frame that might look good with her red hair, and tested them out, blinking a few times and looking around and up to the ceiling. A filigree web swung across from the light bulb to the left corner, where a spider was actually devouring a fly; and a few inches below she noticed a trail of ants traversing a desert of wall, shouldering tiny burdens of sugar; low down in the corner by the counter reclined a fat gecko. It blinked.

'Incredible,' she murmured. 'My other glasses were not as good as this.' She picked up a magazine from the rack by the counter and flipped it open. The text jumped out from the page, dark and sharp: Tropical ants that nest in forest canopies launch into the air to avoid predators, then glide back using their legs as rudders, scientists have found.

'I'll take these,' she said, turning to the girl at the till. 'I like them. They're very clear.'

The girl's eyes were somewhat bulbous and her nose protruded above a sharply receding chin, making Gloria think of a grasshopper. *Proboscis.* The word leapt into her mind as she paid over the small sum of $5. The woman who had been browsing among the men's jackets and trousers was sidling near on her right, watching. Gloria took the small bag from the salesgirl and turned away towards the door—and suddenly the woman was there too, determined to talk. Gloria smiled weakly and reached for the door. It tinkled as she opened it and clicked shut behind her. She was pleased with her glasses; the world was clearer and better focused.

'Excuse me!' She turned at the voice behind her. It was the browsing woman again, the one from the shop, standing there, stocky and insistent, steel grey hair cut short and square—older than me, thought Gloria—grey eyes keen behind rimless spectacles and smiling slyly like a naughty child.

'I just wanted you to know you've got my husband's glasses,' she said, edging forward. Her voice was high and child-like.

Gloria clutched the brown paper bag more tightly, pulling back.

'I mean, I'm glad it's you,' she said. 'You look the right sort.'

'Oh?' Gloria countered. 'As long as they do what I want.'

'Oh they *will*, they *will!*' the woman exclaimed, almost skipping in her enthusiasm and clapping her palms together. 'He'd like you to have them, I know. They were such a *part* of him, never without them. And when you tried them on, you looked just like him!'

Gloria edged away, but the woman was not to be put off. 'He had *such* an interesting way of looking at the world.' She peered in a questioning way at Gloria, as if willing her to ask for an explanation.

'I'm sure you miss him,' Gloria murmured, more tart than sympathetic.

'That's why I come down here.' The woman leaned into Gloria, like a gleeful conspirator. 'Last week, it was his shoes, a really good pair with thick rubber soles. A young man going overseas took them; he'll go far! Can I ask what you do?' Her tone was winsome, beguiling.

'I'm a writer,' Gloria said.

'Isn't that wonderful!' The woman lifted her face to Gloria, smiling again in her strange, sly child's way. 'Now I *know* you are right for them—'

'Look, if you don't mind, I have an appointment,' Gloria said,

45

more tartly than she intended. 'It was nice to have met you.' She wheeled away, affecting urgency as she strode back to the car, but feeling shame at her brusqueness. The woman had meant no harm and was clearly lonely, still grieving. Why had she closed her off? It was becoming a habit, she thought, this extricating from encounters, putting up a wall to let her work on her writing. Perhaps it was why the work had stalled over the last few years—longer really, ever since Martin had left. Even before that—he hadn't wanted to live with a closed door, he said. She had let her life shrink to a dull routine of denial; she'd stopped the part-time tutoring and the historical association; she no longer sang in the choir. She told herself she'd reached 'the settled stage' of life, had given up expectations of adventure, amorous or any other kind. And yet, here she was, only 53: some people—popes and prime ministers—were just beginning careers, even in their seventies; only this morning she'd read of a couple in their eighties getting married...

She was still ruffled when she reached home and she called Bettina to relay her encounter with the spectacle owner's widow. 'And do you know, I have the feeling it's not the last time I'll be seeing her. It's as if she has a proprietary interest in me—now that I'm viewing the world with her husband's gaze!'

'The main thing is; do they work?'

'Oh, wonderfully, and only $5. I've saved hundreds!'

She picked up the battered glasses case, removed the spectacles and put them on. She blinked a few times and almost immediately a thread of ants jumped into focus, spanning the ceiling to the corner above the door, where she noticed a crack and what looked like the dead body of something, a slug perhaps or a moth.

'In fact,' she went on, 'they are amazingly effective. I can even see ants on my ceiling!' She lowered her gaze experimentally to the floor. 'Actually, I see more detail than I really want: oops, there's a daddy-long-legs behind that curtain—and another ant trail. I see I'm going to have to focus on housework more—I'd better go!'

She replaced the receiver thoughtfully. It seemed as if the glasses had a way of foregrounding insect life. She took them off and was relieved by the bland, blameless expanse of familiar wall. She put them on again and stared down at the desk. Ants were there, too, and fly spots on her manuscript; a silver fish slithered out from her *OED*. She spent a few minutes experimenting, raising and lowering the spectacles. It was strange, but the glasses were somehow programmed to pick up insect life.

She noticed, then, a name scrawled across the optician's label under the lid of the case. The writing, spidery in its extensions, was difficult to read: 'B Fill', or 'B Till', perhaps, with a phone number. She wondered about the owner of the glasses. It was ridiculous even to think it, but had he been especially involved with insects in some way? Was it possible that... Or was it simply a question of prescription, of astigmatism or a magnification she was not yet used to? Perhaps she had grown accustomed to not-seeing? It was feasible. She thought again about how closeted her life had become: how, in shutting off, she'd chosen to live in her mind's eye, in distant, imagined pasts of the Classical world. Had she become blind to the life around her? Its seething minutiae, even right under her nose? She thought of going back to the opportunity shop to look for the spectacle widow and asking about her husband. She had seemed a rather interesting and unusual person herself. Perhaps she was someone—but she pushed the thought away: she would work on her novel.

The afternoon passed well, with the writing flowing fast and smooth and a new plot line emerging: Pulcheria, it transpired, had scientific interests drawing her to the study of *Kermes vermilio*, the remarkable insect crushed to make the crimson dye so favoured by Roman court ladies, including Eudocia, her jealous sister-in-law. Opposed to violence in all forms, Pulcheria began a bitter campaign against insecticide and so met the senator Marcian, whom (Gloria has discovered through her historical research) she would eventually marry.

It was impossible to stop writing over the next two weeks. Her work was more detailed than before and involved more research. Pulcheria's campaign was joined by Hypatia, a Greek mathematician and philosopher renowned for her studies of *Scarabaeus sacer*, the Egyptian scarab beetle...

She was careful not to wear her glasses out of the house any more: she had discovered their tendency to exaggerate the bug-like features of those she encountered: the man at the corner shop with his narrow brown termite head, the milkman's busy coleopteric mouthparts, and even Bettina, on a recent visit, rotund in a new polka-dot orange suit, had resembled a lady bird. But she was grateful for the new energy and focus in her writing and as

47

the work neared completion her mind turned again to the woman in the opportunity shop and the man whose vision had inspired her. A search of the Web threw up a conference paper ('Laboratory and field tests of entomopathogenic nematodes against the scarab beetle, *Temnorhynchus baal*', Till, B & Hopper, G.R., 1988), but nothing further.

On an impulse, one early Saturday evening, she called the number scrawled inside the brown spectacle case. The phone rang for a long time and she almost put down the receiver when a woman answered, but not in the high-pitched voice she had remembered from that day outside the opportunity shop.

'I'm looking for Mrs. Till,' Gloria began. 'Mrs. B. Till?'

'Oh, I'm sorry,' the woman replied. 'I'm so very sorry.'

'She's not there, then?' Gloria asked, thinking the apology somewhat effuse. 'Are you a friend?' the woman returned.

'I wanted to speak to her. You see I met her recently and—'

'She's gone. She's passed.'

'Passed?'

'Yes, she died last week. She was holding out for him.'

'I don't understand,' said Gloria.

'Most wouldn't. She was waiting for them to go. His things.'

'Her husband, you mean? Mr. Till?'

'The Professor, such a lovely man. She doted. Hung on, you know, waited till it was all gone. When the tweed jacket went, she said it was the last time.'

'Are you a relative?' Gloria asked.

'She had none, not as far as I know. I work at the op shop on Cricket Road. She came everyday.'

'I bought his spectacles there,' Gloria said. 'They were very helpful. I didn't see you there.'

'My daughter works mornings. Anyway, can I help you with anything?'

'I was just wondering,' she said, 'If you had any more spectacles in the shop?'

'We may have, I don't know. Is it for yourself? I'm tied up right now, sorting through this house. She put my name down, you see, and I have to get rid of all this.' The voice took on an edge of exasperation. 'My daughter's going overseas next week and I've got no one for the shop. May have to close it, for a while at least.'

'That would be a real pity,' Gloria said. She pulled out the green spectacles and put them on again. A cockroach sat blatantly in the middle of the floor; she could swear it was blinking. She glanced out the window at the harbour, the ferry, and the yachts —and saw there were people down there, too, people walking along the sea front, some roller blading, babies in prams, joggers and toddlers. Funny not to have noticed them before, the boys on bicycles or trailing kites... She yearned at once to be a part of it all, to whizz among the throng herself or sit on a bench and chat.

And before she could stop herself, she was saying, 'I could do it. Help you out, I mean—for a few weeks, at least. Perhaps longer —'

Amy Mackelden

Jack's Jumper

Jack's jumper's old wool that's not shrunk yet and that's unusual, but when you don't wash clothes and they weren't washed before you bought them from a vintage shop, a charity shop, a market, they tend to stretch and pull, to hang at the elbows, sag at the neckline, and his earphones are in his pocket, start to fall out of it when he's rummaging for change and Rizlas, and he looks away more often than not, doesn't food shop, has nothing in his cupboards, not even tea bags, and his last phone broke so this one's a ten pound replacement that functions like 2004, and he hasn't laughed in years, not since he moved to the north, and even then, before, I'm not sure he found things funny, that his jaw contorts enough to laugh or smile, and the skin on his back's a shock, a red raw island that stops at his shoulder bones, bends on his ribs, and his posture's not a thing he cares for, wouldn't stand up to shake your hand unless he thought there was money in it, and on a Saturday night he starts by saying he's not going out, that he's got five pounds to last until Sunday, next Sunday, then he goes out anyway, and his teeth seem to bend in bright light, same as the lines he spins like fictional things between 8 a.m. and the evening, and the aftershave Cara bought him before is an empty bottle on the chest of drawers that spill clothes to the floor like they're leaking.

Gems
Snowflake Obsidian

I'm a scalpel; you're shell. We're essentially the same, give or take our water content, the fact we're from a different continent altogether. But there aren't trees where we're from because you're underwater and the sort of plant life you've got's not oak, isn't acorn or horse chestnut. And where I am, this cluster, every tree got cut to make way for carved stone, and it's the sort of precision you could take to bark, could slice and sort rings out, find how old every branch is by the centre of it. But now, each tree's a stump, our volcanoes sunk, the smallpox was rife but now isn't, and I crack: there's no pattern to it. I don't follow graphs because I'm flint, I'm glass, and I scatter, shatter into a hundred tools when you drop me.

11 July was the first full eclipse in 1300 years, and in the changed light you'd find white specks in dark glass, eczema blotches, print from leaning on a bus seat too long, Jack's pillowcase proving your skin's shapeable like sushi, mouldable origami. I'm less than one percent water, and I'm more than nothing, only just, in the way my surface smoothes, the gradual way it curves, breaks and starts, like you. You're mussel shell.

Jack in Slovakian

Oh, Jack. You bring me back from Europe. You drag me back from European capitals. I think I go with you willingly. But they took my language so when we speak it makes no sense. I repeat certain words over like 'Slovenska' and 'sendvič' and 'fish' (but in Slovakian). And your name, Jack. I remember your name.

The whole place was empty. I had mountains and lakes, and patches of land that used to belong to other people. Do you belong to other people, Jack? Have I left it too long? Slovenska never really owned me, Jack. Sure, we saw the same film once, but at separate times. We cried at different bits.

But you, me, Jack. We're barely separate people. We held hands before, in films we weren't meant to be in. We found excuses and we made lists, and you paid even when I became a feminist. And you tried to make me see the right thing. I see that now. But when you're blind, or at least very short-sighted, you see nothing, or very little.

I've got to stop just saying 'Ľúbostný', and instead really show it by my actions.

The first thing I think I should do, Jack, is to stop eating sandwiches with Slovakia. I will stop having lunch with Slovakians.

But this is in Slovakian and you don't speak that.

DIY, or don't

There was a one inch gap where the skirting board stopped and the floor boards started, and in some places you could see to the brick behind, but other spots, not even a hint of the house's anatomy. So I sliced the polystyrene which came casing the dishwasher and wedged it in, wedged it under, piece by piece, to stop drafts, to keep rodents from coming up.

When Jack came round, came in, the first thing he said was, 'What a mess, what clumsy cutting,' and, 'You should've got expandable foam in it.' And then he scanned every room like an X-ray, picking out faults, pointing out breaks, suggesting fixes, and he said, 'I worry for you here. I worry for you both, now. No radiators in the back half, no blind on the back door, holes in the walls where the cable is, and a wonky fire place. And all the doors are too high up so you need excluders and the wires are exposed on all the lighting, and the condensation in the bathroom shows how cold it is, and I won't even start on the boiler being in your bedroom.'

Then he left, leaving half drunk hot chocolate, and the thought of his lips, his saliva that's gluey mint, made me think of leeches, made my mind up. So I slipped polystyrene in the other rooms. I plugged the gaps up, deleted his suggestions. I sent him an email, a text. I said, 'I need more space,' but he doesn't get it.

Lindsey Holland

Hot

is when I tiptoed in wellies
to the kitchen, reached
soil chubby fingers to the oven
and perhaps
dizzied by gingerbread grabbed
the baking tray.
'Under the tap!' you yelled.
The water ran until
the burn felt like ice

but it hurt when you were sleeping
and I flooded the bathroom —
a cold pool creeping
to the door, my hands'
impossible fumbling,
crying on the tap:
'I can't turn it off'.

Hot is the objects I still keep touching
and they are always chased
by water panic deluge.

These things swim

in shoals: kettles and radiators,
trays, pans, gas rings.
They move on currents,
west and then north where they
meet and neutralise
icebergs as though
meltdown is inevitable.

And you are in the garden,
planting carrots, composting,
doing your bit.

Noel Williams

A clear sky. Snowdrifts.

You know that place where four paths meet
near the cemetery's brow, where I gaze sometimes
over the stumps of the common graves
low on the slope, or up to the shadows of angels,
with the ache behind me of the arthritic gate,
and ahead the long sleeping street
of mound after mound swollen, down
to the drop of the valley? There,

as if cupped in the calyx of the city's black flower
I stared into silence, between ice-whitened yews
where two headlights swept up to me,
roving the graves and strobing the drifts
from left to right, so the glide of the beams
lit up one by one each of your words
I'd shaped in the darkness of snow.

Daphne

If I was to call myself un-uprootable
you would measure the dredge
of my feet in the lakeside (where fox-colours
glide just under the glaze). You would
flick through your lexicon of trunks
and branches, testing: am I worm-filled, leaning,
am I wind-fingered and dreaming
with the madness of trees?

You would map my toes' hook, my clutch
of the mud and my sway as I'm stripped
by the wind; want to tap the resins
of surely my leaking vocabulary.
Am I rotted by autumn? Is it a fit?
A despair in the sap that forces
such forging of syllables? To
drill down and anchor, to tree me
where all leaves have dissolved on the lake bed?

If I was to call myself un-uprootable
you'd put your sole to a spade,
you'd whet each blade of your lips.

Of the heart

So you quit the page for the garden
which wears a streetlit kilt of rain.
The twist of your ribs continues.
Whatever nests in that fork of bones
turns and turns like a dog after comfort.

Touch the washing line,
rhinestones strung against the garden's dark.
Raindrops arpeggio down, timed
to the tick ticking of your left arm.
The fall of this aurora, spark by spark,

troubles the mud, like silver silting a vein.

Tishpishti
Joanna Campbell

Dieter pressed his glasses onto the bridge of his nose and looked up at the corduroy vision of Jack Sanderson. They extended hands, Dieter a fraction of a second before his host.

'Well, Dieter,' Jack barked, 'welcome to England. Weather's typical, I'm afraid.'

The rain clattered onto Dieter's leather jacket and streamed over his glasses. He smiled and shook Jack's hand with vigour, jostled by other exchange students and host-families dashing to their cars. He was immovable, a statue set in stone by the weight of his drenched canvas backpack.

'I like this English air. Clean.'

He continued to stand there, elbowed and jogged and dripping. Pumping Jack's long liver-spotted hand.

'Well,' said Jack, irritated, 'let's run for cover. I've brought the grotty car. Sally wants to drive, you see. Got one of your Mercs at home.'

Dieter turned to Sally. She held an umbrella over her long ginger hair. Dieter let his hands drop from Jack's. Although his eyes, little velvet moles dug deep into his face, did not appear to move, they absorbed the plump English hills and rounded valleys of her body within its Mackintosh. They roved without hint of movement up each brow, over all crests and down every slope of her landscape, ending at her eyes, the shade of a yellowing pear and her whipped cream skin. German boys worshipped red hair. Dieter felt its length wrapping around his naked body, a skein of rusty silk, slipping and sliding against him.

'Hello, welcome to England. This is Graham.'

A dark mass of wet quilted nylon behind Sally, Graham hunched into his anorak, hair plastered to his head like the corpse of a drowned field-mouse. He kept his hands in his pockets.

'Graham's the linguist,' Sally said, turning to give her brother a purposeful look. 'Say something,' she hissed at him.

Graham followed his father to the exit.

'Sorry Dad shouts,' Sally continued. 'He thinks you'll understand better. He shouts at us too. Always thinks shouted English is clearer than spoken.'

Dieter sat in the front with Sally, a liver and white Spaniel panting down the back of his neck and an industrial-sized jar of pickled beetroot between his feet. Sally's hair swung in a curtain round the steering-wheel and over the gear-stick. Jack lifted the spaniel's ear to yell through to her.

'Can't you get out of second? Bloody engine's making a hell of a noise.'

The drive was long and jolting. Eruptions of swear words and yelps and grunts from the back-seat added to the strain imposed by the low sky and steamed windows. Dieter rubbed clear patches on the windscreen, but saw only sodden greens and browns like mouldering gingerbread.

'You have a farm, Graham said on his letter, Mr Sanderson,' he said at last, queasy with petrol and damp dog fumes.

'Pig and poultry,' replied Jack.

Sally's hand brushed Dieter's leg as she struggled to push home the recalcitrant gear-stick. His jeans tightened. He shifted on the smooth worn seat. His glasses had become opaque. He polished the lenses on his handkerchief, laying this across his lap when he'd finished.

He thought Sally glanced at him, a dimple in her cheek. He felt Graham's eyes on his back.

The farmhouse smelt as damp as outside. Sally filled the kettle for tea and asked Graham to show Dieter to their room.

'Top bunk's mine,' he said and went downstairs.

Dieter wrinkled his nose at the heap of football gear and plates of brittle crusts. The window was jammed open. Rain splattered the sill. Mildewed curtains billowed, straight and horizontal, into the room, unflinching banners making some kind of protest.

Dieter put his backpack down and sat on the bed. He touched the sheets and a thin blanket. An English bed. And the air that at four o'clock in his country would be spiced with black coffee and plum cake, reeked of blocked toilets.

He looked in the bit of mirror propped on Graham's bookshelf. His face was the colour of weak tea, his thin cheeks hollow with fatigue.

'How old's your father?' Jack had yelled in the car.

The question hung in the stuffy doggy gassy air. Yet something plaintive rang in the core of every syllable. Dieter spoke to the windscreen, to the little oval aperture he'd made with his elbow.

59

'He had been born 1920.'

'Ah. Same as me.'

The statement dangled awkwardly.

'Show you my medal at home. And photos I've got of those years. I'll show you.'

Dieter felt menace. He felt Jack's bread-and-Cheddar breath on the back of his head.

Dieter returned to the landing and leant on the banister overlooking the kitchen.

He saw Sally place a brown cake in a plastic wrapper on the table. Jack set the places and took the bread slices out of the packet. They dusted the better cups that hung from hooks on the dresser. Pots of jam gathered on a tin tray.

Dieter joined them at the table. He peered at the jam when Jack shoved the tray towards him. Sally sat next to Dieter, scraping her chair in close until her breasts rested on her plate.

'Mum made a huge batch before she went to the hospice. The labels were the last things she wrote. Greengage, gooseberry, loganberry. How do we say those in German?'

Graham picked up a jar and smoothed a thin finger over the label, shadowing the path of his mother's hand all those dark months ago.

Sally buttered a slice of bread. It looked pale to Dieter, used to dark rye and caraway crusts.

'Tea-times don't smell right now,' she said. 'When Mum was alive, an almond cake, drenched in honey and all stiff with nuts, always sat in the middle of the table. Now we buy things in packets.'

Jack and Graham didn't speak.

Dieter noticed Sally staring at an apron hanging by the range, looped on a nail in the stone wall. He imagined the mother's hand on the nail, palm pressing on the metal head, the last time she hung it there. As if she tried to imprint this final maternal act on her flesh. Now the sun was bleaching the puffy folds of the apron to a frail yellow.

'We have breads and cake at our home,' Dieter said. 'Different kinds. But we have the almond and honey Kuchen.'

A breeze dashed in. The Venetian blind clacked. The sun that had striped the table and glanced on the glass of the gun-cupboard, vanished.

Dieter listened to the laboured progress of the clock on the wall. Rain hurtled down again. He heard the distant squawk of chickens seeking cover. The kitchen grew so dark that all he could see were shadows sitting at the table.

'What's your father's line of work?' Jack added an inch of whisky to his tea.

'You have honey and almond cake at your home?' Graham spoke for the first time.

The tip of Dieter's tongue licked at the Marmite on his crumpet.

'My father is a carpenter. And, yes, we eat Tishpishti.'

Sally gasped. Jack stared at Dieter and augmented his tea with more whisky, not even looking at the bottle and cup, letting the scotch flow into the saucer, where it drowned a woodlouse.

Graham looked down at his plate. His finger traced a line through the scattered crumbs.

Sally cleared her throat.

'Dieter, would you happen to be Jewish?'

'Yes, Sally. That is correct. In fact, half-Jewish on my mother's part.'

Jack snapped a lamp on. Faces became black and amber masks, illuminated under cheekbones, eyes obscured in deep sockets.

Jack's crusty beard splayed out from his face.

As dusk fell, rain still teemed. Sally showed Dieter the barn. He giggled, unsteady and leaning on her a little as they climbed the ladder to the hay-loft.

'Am I now less a threat to your father?'

'Think so. He was a bit afraid of you before, I think.'

'I like his scotch whisky.'

'We can sort of slide down over the bales. It's a lot of fun. A bit prickly and bumpy. Come on, I'll hold your hand.'

They slid together, landing in unbaled hay lit by a finger of moon. Dieter listened to Sally's laughter, his legs tangled with hers and his head against her arm. The flesh exposed by her shrunken, faded countryside clothes lived its own separate life. Her body was now his home.

Their breath fanned out, smoky in the raw air.

Dieter had seen his host snoring in a chair by the dying fire and Graham holding a photograph in the scullery.

Dieter's mother had told him to accept hospitality with

gracious appreciation. He accepted Sally's by slowly, politely, rolling her jeans down to her ankles.

Clinking bottles made their way up the backstairs from the cellar every evening.

'Pity you don't know more about your father's war record. Get him to write to me when you're back.'

'You do not mind him being, how do I say it, on the opposing side?'

'Soldiering is soldiering, boy. Soldiers serve. They take orders and they carry them out.'

Dieter brushed his lips with his glass, waiting for Jack to break down and sink into sleep.

'When I had to raise my gun, my thought was always this, Dieter. That young soldier is just like me. He has a mother too.'

Sally stoked the fire. Dieter watched her disturb the sleeping logs, blow life into the tongues of flame. As the fire roared, Jack seized his sleeve to pull him close.

'Your father would have felt just the same. A good soldier does his duty. Doesn't feel hatred. The enemy stands on the other side, but his heart's beating the same rhythm.'

Sally suggested taking the dog out, locking the chickens in. She could hear foxes at night, padding through the soaking fields, brazen, seeking. She took down her raincoat from the peg.

'Dieter, your father and I are soul-mates. Both married Jewish ladies. I wish Hannah could make Tishpishti for you now. You'd feel right at home then, boy, I can tell you. Nectar.'

Jack pushed his hands through his hair and leaned his elbows on the table. Dieter stifled a yawn and a glance at Sally.

'Sweet cheese dumplings with sugared berries. That was my favourite. Your mother makes that, I'm sure, Dieter.'

'Mm, sweet, sweet dumplings, Mr Sanderson. I love them so much.'

Dieter stood, one eye on the door, one on Jack's slumping head.

'Hannah suffered you know. God how she suffered.'

Dieter sat down.

'April 1941, it was. At the Jewish Girls Club in West London. Bomb killed twenty-seven of them outright. She saw her sister die. Worse for the people struggling to live their lives. Easier to be a soldier. Our job to sacrifice our lives for their sake. An

Englishman's home is his castle, Dieter. Bet it's the same for you Germans, eh? We all fear invasion.'

Dieter stared, no longer bothered with manners. He wanted to run with the foxes of the night, flee to the barn and taste the sweet meat of his host's daughter, gnaw on the forbidden flesh. His fortnight was almost over. The feast was coming to an end.

Jack's head dropped onto his arms. Sally and Dieter ran into the cool damp air.

Later, she rested her head on his chest.

'Graham hasn't improved his German. Hasn't even tried, the little sod. Hardly uttered two words to you.'

'Why did he bother to take part in the exchange? He didn't want a student from my country here,' Dieter mused, running a finger through her red fringe.

'A boy in his class dropped out. So you were surplus to requirements. Graham had his arm twisted. School said it would do him good. Bring him out of himself.'

Dieter lit a cigarette. Sally glowed in the flare from his match.

'Well, my dear Sally, at least you have learnt much from me.'

She giggled through her tears.

'I feel sort of unfettered with you,' she said

'Unfettered? What is that? Like a bald baby bird?'

'That's unfeathered. Come to think of it, I'm a fledgling. Learning how to be without my mother.'

'Tell you what,' he said, swigging the last of Jack's latest bottle, 'my mother isn't Jewish at all.'

A tear sloped onto Sally's lip and he kissed it with practised tenderness.

'I eat Tishpishti at a friend's house.'

Sally sat up, the hay rustling gently as she moved.

'I heard something,' she whispered.

'Foxes,' he said, grazing the tip of her nipple with his tongue.

'No.'

'What else?'

'Footsteps, I think.'

'You panic.'

Sally tried to lie down for the last time in the damp barn.

'And my father was a conscientious objector. No medal for him. They put him in a psychiatric hospital. He came out broken. My mother holds him together. That is her life. That is what war does.'

'You lied to get on my father's good side?'

'Indeed, Sally. Better to be on the same side.' He kneaded her thigh. 'What use is there in the truth?'

The door clicked. It dragged open through the piles of strewn hay. A photograph fluttered to the ground.

The shot pierced the silence. Another silence followed. Then the barking of the old dog, the footsteps of Jack running outside from the kitchen chair, the clucking of a hundred terrified chickens and the occasional grunt of a pig disturbed from sleep.

Alex Josephy

Manoeuvres

Don't ride the clutch. Ease up,
you'll ruin the gearbox. Next left
into the side road and we'll try

parallel parking. Indicator.
Right hand down, no, wait,
check the mirror. You were saying

something about a summer night
in France, a quayside bar, insults
in another language, mopeds racing

the wrong way up the fast lane.
For God's sake. But it's all right,
you're telling me, that was two years ago,

it's over, Mum, and you glide to a halt
to wait courteously at the crossing
for an old woman with a shopping trolley.

Elbows on the Table

He's in Tuscany, 1945, alive
in the ruins of a gatehouse.
The room is cold, butter hard
in the dish, and they have on
heavy jumpers. He turns down
a corner, worries a crease
close to the spine, breadcrumbs
cinder-light between the pages.

She's a pirate's child
at the court of the Virgin Queen.
She loves this story already;
it's a parterre of branching paths.
She hops between the box hedges,
picks a sprig of rosemary, reads
the last paragraph first, then a section
from Chapter Two, then starts
in earnest, white pages wheeling
like moths between her palms.

Coffee cools in the chipped enamel jug.
Slices of toast stand in the rack:
unturned pages. He looks up,
looks through her,
then picks up his glasses.

In Another Country

They walked   underwater
where thoughts were bubbles

little   strings   of syntax.
Her heel rasped shell walls

caught   down a crevice
where crabs lurked

tentacles quivered.   He dived
to ease her ankle   free.

On   the terrace   she filled the gaps
between olive and oleander

with a hovering paintbrush.
Wine splashed the tiles

his jagging elbow   writing postcards
foreign words   that curved

and   leapt across the page
. dolphins   heading for open   sea.

Anne Hine

Interior with Woman at Piano Strangarde 30 Vilhelm Hammershoi

Again he demands I sit:
without clearing the table
without seeing my face
he must paint me now, at the piano
with my back to him once more.
He hates being watched.

The ebony and ivory beneath my fingers
I play my anger out.
This once serene room filled
with sound, both dark and light.
He will not speak.

The sun does not shine in this morning room
I thunder on, make the pictures rattle,
elbows tight against my waist
the scratch of bombazine lost
in this sumptuous racket.
He is unmoved.

The chair's fan-back supports me
as I rock, use the pedals,
play myself to harmony
find my interior serenity.
He paints on.

Margaret Wilmot

The Butterfly Effect
for Nick and his butterfly

I heard *Monarch* for *Monach* as a seal
rolled high in the curve of a wave

and marvelled that sea-battered islands far west of Scotland
should share a name with butterflies
in another Far West.

Do they still flutter among the lacy fennel on Summer Street?

The sea beats against our screen, spatters.
The drops feel wet.

Huge seal bodies loll weightless in sea-light.

Sunlight trembles through wings fragile as sunset.

The Banished
Tricia Durdey

'Surely you'll not be going out in this fierce weather. It's fit to freeze the cattle.' Sister Helen addressed Sister Dolores, her face silly with devotion.

'Neither flood nor snow will stop me.' Sister Dolores pulled on her outdoor boots, her chapped fingers faltering over the laces.

'You've been coughing all day... you're sick... surely Our Lord would understand...'

'Would you know the mind of God?'

Sister Helen lowered her eyes.

'I'll keep the fire going... I'll make certain...'

'That would be a kindness.'

Sister Dolores closed the convent door behind her and stepped out into the courtyard. The icy wind sweeping around the edge of the building rushed to meet her, but she bent her body low and walked into it. The weather would not prevent her from visiting the Holy Shrine, though the water might freeze on her lips.

It had snowed and settled that morning. With the first flakes the younger convent school girls sitting at break rushed to the windows. It rarely snowed in the west of Ireland and their excited voices rang out across the hall, until Sister Dolores called them to order, striking Susan Mahoney on the back as she ran past. That bold red head needed subduing.

There were few people out on the main street now. The ice clung to the lintels and ledges of the granite church. Declan Foyle trudged towards her on the way to the pub, his head shrunk beneath swathes of scarf.

'A terrible evening sister. You'll not be going far on a night like this!'

She didn't answer, but looked beyond him to the edge of town. The sweet smelling turf smoke buffeted from the chimneys and was carried off into the white air. In the night the lake would freeze, the bog at the foot of the mountain would stiffen. The girls would want to go sledging in the fields tomorrow. The slightest change in routine and they were wild and close to uncontrollable. She would have to stamp them down.

The afternoon light faded and she kept walking, her rosary

beads smooth under the fingers of her right hand. She passed the lighted kitchen window of Murphy's farm and turned between the stone gate posts towards the shrine.

The Holy Mother with her halo of pale neon gazed down at her. Sister Dolores knelt on the stone step, head bowed. Below her the water bubbled from the spring. Hands shaking, she took the metal beaker from the stone wall and dipped it into the water and drank. Ice struck her throat, her gums, the bone behind her eyes. She gasped and dropped the beaker. It clattered on stone. There was an echo, then silence. She began to pray.

'Hail Holy Queen, Mother of Mercy, our Life, our Sweetness and our Hope, To Thee we cry, poor banished children of Eve...'

She blacked out, but the cold brought her back, and she found herself lying face down on moss and dead leaves. She began to shake, a deep tremor that began in her heart and moved out through her ribs, to her arms and legs. She had no control. Over and over again she whispered, 'to thee we cry poor banished children of Eve, poor banished children of Eve... sweet Mary be with me... speak to me, speak to me... I have tried to obey; I have tried to do the will of God...'

She dragged herself towards the candle burning in the alcove at the feet of Mary.

There was a voice.

'Walk, Annie,' the voice told her. 'Get up and walk.'

She crouched by the shrine, trembling, waiting.

Go to the lake at the foot of the mountain. You will find me there.'

She knew then that it was the voice of God.

Fourteen years old Nuala O'Riordan couldn't remember the last time there had been a fall of snow, followed by deep frost. The town looked new, so different from the days of grey mist and drizzle that made the west of Ireland's winter. She sat feeding her tiny son, beside the stove. The coffee bubbled beside her and the baby tugging at her sore breast made her melancholy. Since Matthew was born the world was alien and she herself a stranger. But the snow brought lightness to the sky, as if there was more space, everything wiped clean. Perhaps if Matthew slept well that afternoon she could leave him with her mother and go out sledging with Kathleen Murphy.

Her mother came in laden with washed sheets and peered over

71

at her grandson.

'Ah, he's fallen asleep Nuala, go to Mrs Linehan's for the flour. I'll take him a while.'

Carefully Nuala pulled herself away from the baby's warm slack mouth. He stirred and sighed and settled back down to sleep, his arms flung over his head.

'Lord bless him,' her mother said, looking down at his flushed milky face.

Nuala pulled her coat around her, and made her way down the street to Mrs Linehan's shop. She hoped nobody else would be in the shop—it was horrible the way some people looked at her now. But it was a delight to be outside in this new world whose sky threatened more snow later on. It was as if she felt a shadow on her skin where her son had lain, but she was free and alone now. She stretched and breathed in the cold air.

The bell rang as she pushed open the shop door. It was dark inside. Kitty Devine was there before her. She could hear her strident voice.

'To be sure it's a terrible thing. Whatever possessed the poor lamb.' Kitty's eyes sparkled, then seeing Nuala she fell silent. She piled her provisions into her string bag. 'I'll not keep you now. I'll catch up with you later, Mrs Linehan. '

'What is it? What's happened?' Nuala asked as the door closed on Kitty Devine.

Mrs Linehan leaned towards her.

'Sister Dolores. She went out last night to the Holy Shrine. She never came back. This desperate weather!'

'Why?'

'The Holy Mother alone knows what she was doing out there on her own. They're searching now. She could have died out there, with no-one to pray for her.'

Her voice was shrill with excitement.

Nuala shouted from the hall before she'd pulled off her boots.

'Mammy, Daddy, have you heard the news?'

'You're bringing the cold in and you'll wake the baby! Shut the door.'

Her mother looked up from the ironing. Her father was sitting beside the range in his shirt sleeves, reading the paper.

'Calm down child. Tell us when you've drawn breath.'

But Nuala could not wait. She told them what she'd heard.

'Holy Bloody Mary!' her father exclaimed.

'Michael! Show some respect!'

Nuala glanced at her mother. She felt she ought to cross herself, pray for the poor woman's soul, but instead she started to giggle.

'Mrs Linehan said she just went out walking. Why would she walk Daddy, in this cold?'

He looked at her sidelong. There was mischief in his face.

'Now how would I know the ways of the nuns? Perhaps she's gone to the fairies!'

Nuala dared not look at him again for fear she'd laugh.

'Or she's gone to the bar with Father Mulhany.'

Then Nuala collapsed hysterical with laughter on the sofa.

'Nuala, stop this foolishness.'

'But it's funny the thought of Sister Dolores in a bar, Mammy, having a drink with the priests.' Nuala began to cry. 'I hate her.'

'Oh child! She's a poor bitter woman who's never known love. She not worth your hating.'

Her mother put down the iron and gazed at her daughter. The baby stirred and whimpered.

'She's cruel and horrible. You don't know how horrible she was to me. And I always tried to be good.' She was crying like a little girl now.

'Oh Nuala!' Her mother sat at her side and stroked her damp hair.

The last time Nuala went out before Matthew was born was just before Christmas. She'd gone down to Murphy's farm to collect the goose. It was dusk, a fine rain in the air. The light was on in the yard and she gazed around as she waited for Murphy's boys to come. In a wooden pen six white geese waited to be slaughtered. Mud, straw and feathers lay in puddles at her feet and the wall beside her was spattered with blood. She shivered and wished they would come soon. Someone was shouting from the other side of the farm but nobody appeared. Instead the long stooped figure of Sister Dolores turned the corner of the track leading from the shrine. Nuala shrank back, but the nun had caught sight of her. Sister Dolores didn't walk on by, nor did she call out good-evening. Instead she strode into the yard, her boots splashing through the mud. She stopped in front of Nuala.

73

'Nuala O'Riordan, never forget this. You're unclean and you carry the evidence in your belly. The stain will not be washed away. Never.'

Her voice was shrill as if madness had taken hold of her. Nuala backed towards the wall.

'I lit candles,' Nuala said. The nuns face was so close it frightened her. 'I know you meant me only to light the few, but I thought if only I lit them all... that's why I did it, for my sin. '

'What are you talking about?'

Sister Dolores gripped her head and rubbed her hair in the blood that stained the wall. Nuala could smell the antiseptic of her breath. She tried to struggle out of her hands. 'There. It's good enough for you!'

Then she stopped abruptly, let her go and stared into her eyes.

'I prayed to Our Lady,' Nuala shouted. 'I prayed to be married for the baby's sake...'

A look of pity crossed Sister Dolores face.

'You fool. You've no chance of marriage now.'

'But he will come back for me. I lit candles, I prayed.'

The nun laughed.

'And I tell you that boy will no more come back than you'll be visited by the Angel Gabriel.'

Then, bolder than she'd ever been, Nuala shouted back.

'Then God is useless. You and all of you in your black clothes with your prayers and your rules and your horrible God, are useless.'

Nuala never collected the goose. She stumbled home sobbing in the dark. She let herself into the house through the front door so nobody would hear from the kitchen and she ran up to her room.

Downstairs her mother was making tea. She heard the clattering of pots and her father shouting something, but that familiar world was gone. On her bed she howled until she was exhausted. He would not come. Brendan would never come back and she would have his baby alone and people would shut her out and whisper and shun her in the street until she died.

There was a deep, dull ache in her belly. She sat up, her weakness turned to fury. She tore a fresh piece of paper from her Scripture book. On it she made a line drawing of the mountain and the lake and a huge winged figure, the Angel of Death, shaded in black felt pen. Underneath she drew the nun, a tiny pin figure with the words 'Sister Dolores' written in red. Then she struck a match and let the flame lick the paper until it burst into a blaze. She opened the window and threw it burning into the cold.

Nuala and her friend, Kathleen Murphy pulled a sledge along the frozen track to the lake. Nuala's son was sleeping between feeds and her mother had told her to go, to put colour back in her cheeks. Soon dusk would fall. Breathless they dragged the sledge to the fields at the foot of the mountain, then clambered on. Nuala clutched Kathleen around her waist, then pushed off with her feet. The sledge skittered down the shallow slope then gathered speed, bouncing over the snow to the edge of the lake below.

'Tis great, like flying.' Nuala stretched out her arms to meet the few flakes of snow that twirled in the air, her head thrown back against the cold, her long dark hair caught under her scarf.

Tirelessly they dragged the sledge to the top of the field and sped down, over and over again.

'Let's go higher.'

They sped down faster, until the sledge stopped only just short of the ice.

Sister Helen was standing at the edge of the lake under the pine trees. With aching sorrow she watched Nuala and Kathleen sledging. They were always together. She'd taught them music for two years. The O'Riordan girl who'd had the baby could sing. The girls in her music class terrorised her and she dreaded each lesson, but this child was always gentle and willing to please. She remembered her dreamy face and her clear light voice filling the room.

She wanted to be like Nuala; free and young, with life ahead of her. She wanted to be released from the burden of God, to have a family, a baby. But it was too late now. There had been no-one. Just the charity of strangers, and religion. Then there was Sister Dolores.

'We cannot be friends, it's not a possibility,' Sister Dolores said. 'There must be no special relationship between us.' But by then they were friends already. The rules made no difference, to Helen's love. When she had flu and been dangerously ill, she saw Sister Dolores bending over her bed, a strange light in her eyes. It was as if an angel had entered the room, taken her hand and

75

stroked her forehead. She heard singing from far away. Warmth filled the room with a golden light. Surely love was God given—why would God deny such happiness? Surely love for anyone was beautiful? But Sister Dolores' God said 'Thou Shalt Not,' and she had obeyed.

'Good evening Sister.' The girls walked past her dragging the sledge behind them, their arms linked.

She couldn't answer.

'Sister Helen was crying.' Nuala stopped when they reached the gate to the road. The cattle huddled around the straw beside the hedge and the lights of Murphy's farm welcomed them. The first star had risen in the dusk blue sky. 'We should go see she's all right.'

'I didn't see her crying.' Kathleen carried on walking. 'I'm gasping for tea, come on back.' But Nuala wouldn't go on.

'Take the sledge. I'll not be long.'

She ran along the path between the trees, skirting the bog. It was getting dark now and she couldn't see Sister Helen. She surely couldn't have gone without passing them. She reached the last tree and stopped. She heard the owl and the answering cry and stared out across the white expanse of the frozen lake. There was the frail figure of the nun on the ice, moving slowly further and further away from the shore. Nuala started to walk towards her, but the ice creaked and she was afraid.

'Sister Helen.'

The nun stopped and turned. She had walked far.

'It's not safe.'

She could see her white face, her small hunched body, but she didn't move back towards the shore.

'Be careful.' She felt milk flood her breasts, the heat and tingling. She had to get back to Matthew, but she couldn't leave yet. She inched forward, she kept calling, she reached out her hand.

She saw Sister Helen fall to her knees on the ice. Her cry was like the anguish of cattle when their calves are taken. She rocked and she wailed and Nuala, forgetting all fear, ran skittering towards her. Then she stopped. Sister Helen's hands were pressed to the ice, and there, beneath her was the dark frozen form of Sister Dolores, her veil trapped on the surface, the skin of her face bloated and blue, her eyes like pale marbles.

Nuala screamed until the men came running from Murphy's farm and found them both standing, rigid with horror, on the lake.

The thaw came and the rain fell. Black water dripped from winter trees, from the mossy walls and iron gate of the cemetery. It seeped into the earth, over the newly formed grave of Sister Dolores. As night fell Sister Helen walked alone, from the church, to the graveside, back through the town, passing Declan Foyle as he shuffled from the doorway of O'Connell's bar.

'Goodnight to ye Sister.' He touched the brim of his cap.

Nicola Warwick

Roe

First, you gave me a sighting—
you, in a field at midday, head down and grazing,
primed, when you saw me, to take flight
and reinhabit the forest.

I pined for you, poised at the crown of the hill
against the softening sky of dusk, longed
for you to scatter traces of yourself
that I could find and savour.

By day, I tracked you, interrogating
the ground for a trail of slots, clues
to where you paused to scent the air and listen
before you danced and skittered into cover.

I frisked the branches for snatches
of russet fur, combed the undergrowth
to identify the place where you spent
the night, wanting to lie down in your warmth.

All you'd left me were marks on trees, the places
where you'd browsed and stripped the bark
In evening's mellow light, I dressed
in shades of stealth and set out,

quiet as a tigress, to hide in the land, downwind
from where you haunt. I scattered sweetmeats
and apples to draw you in, held my breath till all I heard
was the throb of an ancient oak against my back.

After the Fall

When she came back
I knew that she was changed
from her walk, how she held herself,
shoulders hunched, an arm
wrapped across her chest
where before she had walked free.

There was something about
the grasses tangled in her hair,
the catch of a petal on her cheek,
grazes where she must have knelt
or crawled on hard ground.

And there was something about her voice,
a darkness that could only come
with rage, her face cast
with a sadness that seemed
to overwhelm her.

Just as I had given every creature
a name, new words formed in my mouth:
immoral, disgrace, shame
and others I had yet
to learn the sense of.

I put up my hand to wipe
a tear that sat on her face
like the dew. Her eyes caught mine
and I was lost in the ache of this;
felt a hot fire slide between two ribs.

As I took it all in,
tried to guess which fearsome beast
she had encountered, which
of the creations she could have crossed,
she held out a hand to me,
said *Do not be afraid,*
our fingers touched and I was ignited.

A Fine Winter

That was a fine winter.
Overnight, frost inched
below ground,
turned the landscape to tundra.
The river stood opaque.
I began to fear
for the small things beneath,
fish silvered and still
as sculptures.

Trees were ebony outlines on the horizon.
The sky was glacier blue
or snow-heavy grey.
Birds were flickers in hedgerows
as they plunged for cover
from the sparrowhawk.

Swans cruised in from the Arctic,
the barn owl's dusk-quartering
marked the end of each day.

I swaddled my hands
in thick mittens, cosy
as wrens huddled in a nest-box.
The badger snored in his sett.
Roots of aconite and violet
stirred to birth their green.

My fingers began to lose
the corpse-white of cold, began to warm
through and blush rose,
heated by a desire to touch.

The Loulan Beauty

I have waited a wealth of years for you,
counted the centuries since I lay down to rest,
knew there would be a you to find me.

You cannot help but be drawn to me.
Your shadow eclipses my outline,
your flesh obscures my winnowed form,
the ghost of me overlaid with sand for you to excavate.

Look at me—brush each grain from my face
but take care. Your hands tremble and scatter dust
over me, as if you're trying to send me back,
to undiscover me.

Look at me—my time-ravaged skin,
desiccated as old leather, aged and ageless,
your ancient seductress, most alluring
in her glittered coat of sand.

I am light as balsa, the husk of a woman
you could have known, layer on layer of me a mystery,
still wrapped in gaudy cloth, my body circled by grave goods,
food for the next life, a head-piece of jewels,
treasures to help you half-write my tale.

Look at me. Pour water on me. Give me life.
Do not let your fingers rub my skin to powder.
I dare you to drag your gaze from my long-lost, gorgon eyes.

Larghetto
Catherine Coldstream

The metronome was still ticking when they found her. It hadn't been long, they said, and the coffee was still warm in the cup. Tepid. Clearing away the debris of years, the accumulated ephemera of more than two decades, Gerald wondered whether it had all been worthwhile. The daily trips to the post office on her behalf, the newsagents' bills, cigarette cards and carefully folded sweet wrappers. Translucent and separated from their metallic linings. Blue, green, pink, each colour coded, like some armoury of redundant generals. All undressed and nowhere to go. The sweets had been eaten.

His fingers fumbled with the pendulum, struck by the fragility of its immediate parts, the narrow resistance of the spine, the awkwardness of readjustment. He'd expected it to slide confidently back into place, was unprepared for the stubborn grittiness of reluctant motion, the grudging jolt at each step like the clicking of so many vertebrae. Not that he'd ever manipulated bone; the touch of ivory was unfamiliar to him beyond occasional contact with Lydia's piano keys. And these he'd never associated with body parts. Black and white. Patterns, chess boards, scales. But these segments were dry, and as stiff as he imagined she must be, slumped in that heavy chair, motionless under shawls, eyes fixed on the ceiling. Carefully he directed the resistant weight back to base, through Andante and Allegretto to Prestissimo, paradoxically the position of repose, at 208 per minute. She'd set it at Larghetto, 56, like a too-slow pulse.

Gerald had helped Lydia for years. Originally little more than a caretaker, he had come to Waverley through the columns of a quaint, now obsolete, local journal, settling into her large house, mastering the secrets of her estate and feeling his way into its hidden crannies, its darkened secrets, as the years had passed. He had quickly won her confidence, with his broad grin and huge, capable hands, graduating from useful to indispensable, predicting her every thought, anticipating her slightest need. Her own fingers, while still agile and knowing in musical motion, pre-programmed to thrill from years of training ('I've been drilled' she would say, 'discipline, it always pays off') had become incapable of any but the most familiar routines. Light switches, door knobs, toothbrushes. But anything trickier was left to her assistant. He knew how to change a fuse and a thing or two about wires and drains. Was practical. She'd laughed at her own helplessness, throwing back silky, mauve-tinted curls as she rocked, the effort straining at the neglected waistline, bangles chiming at her wrist.

But now she was gone and the house was heaving from the shock, the village gossiping. Gerald, a simple man he liked to think, had been entrusted with more than his fair share of duties as a result of recent events, many of them beyond the scope of his previous experience. How to choose the hymns and advise the flower arrangers? Where to find the right sort of coffin and of what design and fabric should it be? A classic model, probably, although he toyed with the minimalism of wicker, the possibility of a donation to a favourite charity. Of the food alone was he confident; duck terrine and a large buffet of fresh salmon salad. Fruit and ice cream to follow. Keep it simple. But he'd never dealt with undertakers before and was feeling nervous, ill-prepared. His hands kept toying, aimlessly, with the heavy signet ring he never took off, the gift of a generous, unknown uncle, a fixture upon his bodily existence, as were the single gold filling and the now faded, well-concealed tattoo. He needed advice and a walk to clear his head. Once this business was over he'd go on holiday (he would surely be a beneficiary) and then face the question of his future.

The gin was open on the sideboard when the women from the village arrived, three lemon wedges bleeding onto a pale blue saucer, no sign of tonic, only the aromatic whiff of marinated juniper. And the remains of fish from last night's dinner. She had been in good form and delighted the guests with Chopin Nocturnes before trailing off into one of her habitual reveries, eyes glazed over, as she seemed destined to remain fixed in his mind, perennially petrified against chintz. The angle of her nose, the characteristic sideways turn of her shoulder, now he came to examine them at close quarters, were unusual. Her features and her posture strained, as though greeting an invisible audience. He had never seen such poise nor met such tastefully muted flamboyance in anyone before. Her hold on him, a younger man (after all) had been unique. Hearing them bustle their way purposefully into the hall, Esther, Lesley and Gillian, armed with goodwill and a clutch of brightly coloured feather dusters, he drained his glass and replaced the lid on the bottle. No good to be seen drinking at this hour. One of them was already weaving her way meaningfully towards the drawing room door, detained only by a momentary glance at the open pages of a gardening magazine. The others were receding, making noises, distant murmurings about tea and the necessity of refreshment. A kettle somewhere was switched on.

Five miles away a curtain twitched and a telephone rang. Fingers were doing the walking as columns were perused, numbers double-checked. Meetings had been arranged at Cramond Bay, a couple of men, briefcases and leather gloves. Holdalls and hatchback cars. Back in Waverley, quiet was creeping over the village, as the news seeped out through shopping baskets and half-closed lips, as observations were made about the weather. The price of eggs had risen. Once again.

Gerald touched Lydia one last time, tender in his recognition of her heavy, worn fragility, uncomprehending at the inexplicable vacancy of familiar features. Newly immobile, she seemed anchored, as though by some invisible burden, a virtual magnetism pulling her towards the tidy turf of palely sage-green carpet. Although absent, she sagged, half-erect among floral furnishings. The peripheral autumnal paisley, once so nearly appropriate, now breathed too heavily, oppressively close with its weaving tendrils, its twisted, enclosing leaves, floor-length drapes around sash windows that had never been opened. The room was suddenly a prison, a cage, unbearable in this heat. Tracing the lines around her mouth, still coral pink and fragranced, he wondered about her quiet dedication, her music, her obsessiveness. Her collections of unusable objects. He wondered whether it had all been worthwhile.

'Waverley seven-three-seven.' He heard the voice of Gillian, fresh-faced from the kitchen, doing efficiency as reassuringly as she could. 'The nephews are all in New Zealand, but we are taking steps to contact them ourselves.' She halted to listen, wiping her hands on the soggiest patch of a smeared, white apron. 'And the nieces, yes, messages have been left already.' There was a finality in her voice; she had the pastry and the dusting to do. Noises-off suggested progress was being made in other quarters, the opening and closing of windows, the sounds of spray and the heady scent of chemical polish. Once the family, if that is what this disparate

84

collection of distant relatives could be called, was contacted and informed, there were the legal issues to be negotiated. No, there were no children, Miss Jacobson had never married. And so it went on, Gerald, standing alone among the armchairs, thought sadly, smiling to himself. There were just her unusual albums and mementoes to be dealt with.

Lydia Jacobson had been a brilliant child, daughter of refugees from the continent, originally of Semitic stock. After a period in Totteridge and a transient brush with fame at the Royal Academy, she had moved to the colonies but returned less than a decade later, disappointed in love. People spoke of an unwanted daughter, of the observable signs of guilt, donations to numerous charities and an orphanage overseas. People spoke. Gerald, knowing more than was proper for a man of his station, cut his nails clean, tended a neat moustache and kept his own counsel, loyal and modest in faded tweed. Creeping upstairs, he went in search of his address book. The fish, now stinking, its partial, twisted skeleton, untouched on the table beside peas, could be dealt with later, by one of the women. He had other, more important things to do. The selection of a black suit, the intricacies of mourning rites, and the impending liturgical dealings with the vicar. It was almost midday by the time he came down again.

'Yes, we can do that for you, certainly,' the officious tone of provincial professionals grated, as Gerald pulled the soft-sucked pencil stub from behind his ear to note down the costs of flowers, the quantities of sandwiches, the colour of the napkins. Canon Bradley had been out and he'd been occupied in a barrage of left messages and crossed lines, automated answering machines that he resented. But now he was making strides, heading for the garage, actively planning the next three moves on the mental chess-board of his looming agenda. He savoured each transaction as a job well done and looked forward to a quiet evening with beer, by the coast, the hurdles of the day behind him. He had a lot to think about, his own future not least, and wanted to be done with all this fuss, the dealing with strangers, the domestic uncertainties, the smell of too much polish.

It was only when he was half way to Cramond Bay that the warden realised he had forgotten something, his hand rigid on the warm and slippery gear-stick. Perhaps it was too late to go back? He had a limited time plan, and could not afford to be late.

Deciding on nonchalance, Gerald drove onwards, all thoughts of his domestic responsibilities receding. He needed this break, as he needed, too, to make these connections, attend these meetings. There were people out there who cared, for whom this was important. He would not drive fast, just at a comfortable pace, a Larghetto, as she once would have said. He would enjoy the views. Coming in sight of the cove he could make out the outlines of the two men, black and straight against the yellow mobility of sand. He had what they would be waiting for, had had it all along, sewn snug into the linings of a rarely worn jacket. It was nothing of material value, only paper, pen and ink. Paper and information. This he could part with now; he had no further need of false securities. He released his hand from the wheel, stretched, and pushed down hard. For a moment he would allow himself to go faster.

Once the women had left and the flurry of intrusion had abated, the silence of the drawing room closed the caretaker in once again, quiet like a slow congealing sauce, a waxy heaviness seeping into the spaces between his thoughts. Something stagnant seemed to fill his nostrils, block his movements, holding him captive as he tasted the weight of the house without her. The weight of stillness. The silence of the piano keys irked him and he touched their grainy, faint-ridged surface with the tip of a bulging forefinger, in a slow caress that tasted of trespass. He was an earthy man, a practical person, who had never allowed himself to be taught the finer things in life. Lydia's music had been enough for him; he'd enjoyed her achievements purely vicariously. Or did he mean platonically? The vicar had been asking him something about this, but he'd shrugged and made some comments about the coffee urn, moved on to the ever familiar territory surrounding refreshments. Jammie Dodgers or Rich Tea.

Glad that the fish had been cleared away, and all evidence of over-indulgence removed, Gerald began to prepare himself for bed. His first night without his mistress. He had taken care of her, as she had of him, and was now redundant. Somewhere there would be a will, the professionals were dealing with that and he would receive a recognition of his dues. About the other stuff, no-one would ever know. He had seen to that too, and was quietly confident of a peaceful retirement, somewhere nearer the coast, but no so far away as to forget. For he would never forget. She had left an indelible mark, her fingers, ever agile, had thrilled and teased him into second boyhood. She had brought him back to life, had given him a purpose.

The piles of music had been bundled into boxes, the metronome, jammed shut at an awkward angle, packed with other accessories into a capacious trunk, the sort people used for going travelling in the days of colonial decadence. Large coloured stamps with exotic place names on its surface. Jamaica and Gibraltar. Progress had been made in disposing of inconvenient items, donations and bequeathments had been executed. The piano would be advertised in the columns of The Lady, no appropriate recipient being found among her immediate circle. As a musician she had been very much alone. Gerald had noted down some important numbers, posted some letters, eaten a solitary light supper and satisfied himself that all the arrangements were in order. His tea had grown cold in its scalloped, porcelain cup.

He leaned over in his bed for the last time, searched again for the missing papers, the ones he'd left behind, rummaging softly in the upper drawer amongst the Quality Street, the wrappers and the tissues. He knew he'd left them there. There with the ancient diaries, testimony to years of uneventful living. Surely no-one would have found them first, would have thought to look through his personal effects? But finding nothing, he reached lazily for a hazelnut cluster, the taste of sugar before bed an illicit pleasure. He had already brushed his teeth. It was time to turn in for the night.

Outside, the dry leaves rustled. Branches seemed restless with approaching rain. A dog barked beyond the village, and a baby, somewhere, could be heard softly crying. Downstairs, at the door of the house, the door through which the undertakers had passed that afternoon, they were waiting. The men who knew more than he did, the ones who already possessed his secret. They had been waiting for him as they had waited for Lydia. Waiting to creep upstairs and find him. Waiting until the ticking of the clock was all they heard, ticking alone like a too-slow pulse. The telephone lines had been cut. Lydia's secret was safe. Gerald switched off the light. It had not occurred to him that he would ever be found out.

Deb Baker

Compassion
a Christmas poem for Brother Charles Edward

The leaves of rhododendrons
curl in the cold.
Bitter wind, the granite sky
cracks open.
The child is three days old.
The parents? They have nowhere
to stay. Name it: homeless.
Gifts? A baby can't wear smiles
and good wishes.
Cheap plastic diapers. A can
of formula. A forgotten stroller,
the color of mushy peas, one
wheel pointed at the door,
the other at the chapel. A bag
of castoff clothes, worn, but clean,
folded carefully. Given, not lent.
All they'd really wanted? Voices.

Alchemy By Botany

In the tall tangle
at the garden's end,
a ramshackle patch
of Queen Anne's Lace.
We clip some together,
take it home,
put the stems
in glasses of water
with drops
of food coloring.
In the morning
I find you,
barefoot, robed
against the chill,
holding a small
flower up
to the first light
to see blushing
petals, molecules
of color drawn
through xylem.
I see veins
in your wrists,
note the curve
of your neck, bent
to the new day,
your eyes
a transom
to the alchemy
in your brain,
synapses crackling.

Both of us are held
to the golden floor,
heartwood,
spinning in gravity.
I hang on
to one quiet moment
opening in me,
in you, through these
cell walls.

David Olsen

Surface Tension

Molecular tribalism—
the affinity of like for like—
inhibits wetting.

A steel needle floats
on still water's resilient
and resistant skin.

Though less dense,
the tense liquid
repels the dry unlike.

Differences past,
our tentative reunion
is brief but tender.

While awaiting my train,
we're wary and afraid;
much remains unsaid.

A silent meniscus
quivers
above the brim.

Martin Willitts, Jr.

During A Long Journey

The road becomes hypnotic,
speaking of things that are passing;
like sirens, about things pass due ,
like how leaves are collected into soil,
like the clouds take away and give.

You are tight as hands on a steering wheel.

You pull over to rest.
You let the world rush by you
like a flight of restless birds.

You lower the side window.
A breeze from somewhere distant, visits.
It has been waiting just for you.
It always has been waiting for you.

It takes awhile to relax
into the heartbeat around you.
Some things should never be hurried.
Like a seed that takes time
in silent prayer before awakening.

You are under a tree.
You start to wonder what kind of tree it is.
But the name relaxes within you.
You let go of something,
then you let go of everything.
And then the day turns its page on you.

Touch Is Something We All Need

'I love pictures which make me want to stroll in them, if they are landscapes, or caress them, if they are nudes' — Pierre Auguste Renoir

Better yet, I want to caress a landscape.
I want the impact of the translation of light
upon the waves ingrained on a tree bark,
and I want to trace my fingers on those deep furrows
to hear what they have seen all those watchful years.
It is the same as massaging and breaking the tension
like a rise of startled quail, or the break of air at sunrise.
In that tree's branches, trying to hold things still
long enough for us to enjoy seeing them,
a song of a pinfeather, a knit of string and sprigs,
a egg holding its secrets in blue-speckled breathes.

Below, flowers curl as earlobes,
hearing things approach,
waiting for us to inspect them for perfection
like a craftsman with absolute standards.
I want to stroke across the chambers,
like soft-carpeted footsteps
approaching a lover, as if I want to touch
the light in their hair before it fades
and find the undertones.

In the naked light,
everything looks like field sprays,
like dappled skin in transferred light,
like it has been waiting all morning
for us to kiss them with the lightest kiss possible,
not waking up or startling anything,
and still be a kiss. It is waiting for us to find it,
in this exposed moment, that is
if we are not too embarrassed to look.

Look!
—it is blushing as a rose petal in the arousal of light.
How it purrs and stretches, satisfied,
as it slides into awakening.

The Sounds Of Color

'I want a red to be sonorous, to sound like a bell' —*Pierre Augusté Renoir*

There is an effect if light on an object
juxtaposes tints as to make colors alive
and quiver, as if the surface was breathing.
I often hear this, although I am losing my hearing.
I hear color altering—it is not always bells.
Sometimes they warn like crows warring over a carcass.
Sometimes they jangle like cow bells returning.
Sometimes they are water snuggling against a canoe.
Sometimes they haggle over nothing and everything
like at an open bazaar where someone is handling
a silk scarf before wearing on their head.
The sound of color speaks with authoritative words.
They converse with sensuality like a whispering lover
whose words reach inside you, tingling and joyous.
It is not always so tonally red,
although I can read the surface
easily as a capstone or an anecdote of bronze sunsets.
What should you have me make of such intensity?
Such laboring? To gain, what?—heaven?
I am deluged in their songs of praise.
And what should I not be caught up in?—the adoration?
And why should I ignore it, when I can't?
I am a newcomer to these sounds.
Or perhaps, more like a beachcomber
finding what remains when the tides recedes.
When I hear what others do not, I am blessed!
And in this, I am closer to what I need to hear.
Sometimes, it is too much for just one person.
Sometimes, it just begins to be enough.
The red winds of music are bells in my heart ringing.

Sus
Ken Head

Beyond the window
speed reduces landscape
to an afterthought

Soldiers deployed beside the track, tanks slewed in an armoured chicane across a narrow road in the middle of nowhere. More than enough, you'd think, to warn us something wasn't right before our *tgv* throttled back to a resentful stop alongside a deserted forest halt too small to have a name. But nobody reacted until teams of men with scanners and laptops clambered aboard to check passports, slowly, carefully, giving out those small-hours, Cold War frontier vibes that make you wonder, if your memory stretches back that far, what it is they've already decided you've done.

Knowing the doors are locked doesn't help either, not if you're already as jumpy as he was, the man in the single window seat, travelling alone without much luggage. They barely glanced at his passport, dark green, elegant gold lettering on the cover, before they led him away, one of them carrying his bag and looking worried. There'd been no security check at Lausanne station, where we'd all got on, so nervous questions floated in the air.

After an age, they brought him back, watched as he struggled to stow his bag, then left him, humiliated, too shattered to face his own reflection in the window and as close as most men get to tears, to stew over whatever might've been said or done while they'd held him somewhere none of us could see.

For the rest of the journey, he seemed asleep, arms folded across his table, head down, barely moving until we arrived in Paris, where he disappeared, as we all did, quickly, onto the busy concourse. Looking for cover inside the crowd? Trying to blend in, as if he thought he must still be wanted for something?

In suspicious times
mistrust and fear
find everybody guilty

Aisling Tempany

Margaret

In this photo, aged 14
Margaret sits in a pink dress.
You can see her knickers,
they are also pink.

Margaret here is smiling
and holds her sister on her lap.
In this photo, no one knows

That she would run away.
That she'd change her name and her nation.
She'd dye her hair, and put on weight
and never speak to that sister again.

In Avenham Park

We found no fish in the Japanese Garden
They died in the pond years ago
after a misunderstanding over freshwater and salt.

We found the sundial in the shade
where it can't tell the time because of the trees.
There was also the old tram-bridge that we're afraid to cross
because it's so very high, and so very old.
We found the bandstand that nobody plays on.

And we found the police, who sent us away
while they pulled Janet Murgatroyd out of the river.
She was thrown off the railway bridge.

Give me words

Languages in descending order are: Azerbaijaini, Icelandic, German and BSL.

Give me words
so I can say
how I feel,   *Män qämli,*
what I want,   *Þinn ást,*
what I need.   *Ihr liebe.*

I am trapped in silence, dumb.
I want expression.
Give me your hands.   *Right hand closed rested on left palm in formation*
Whatever you can.   *moving forward and back.*
Oh please, please,
give me words.

Jo Hemmant

Give me the boy till he's seven

It was Mother taught me to be a magician. A cabbage, three potatoes, the ghost of a pot roast picked clean on blue and white china from Budapest. A feast for her and my father, seven growing kids.

The first time I swung
on my makeshift trapeze,
executed a back flip
from its hurtling seat

how she said my name, Ehhh-rich,
as if I had taken her life away,
returned it in a new set of clothes,
face cleaned.

The magician's assistant

I can tell you the moment we fell into place
like the perfection of a difficult trick: a kiss
on the cheek, out on the Coney Island boardwalk

that first night. I was trying my luck, leaning in,
whispering with a con man's oily charm
how each star had been lit up just for us, a galaxy

of astrological signs. But as I drew close
something happened I can't explain. Intuition?
Wishful thinking? Clearer than memory;

as choreographed as a stunt, images of the life
we would have hard on one another's heels
like the pages of a flick book ticking. A wave

hitting the sea wall brought me back, a cold shower
of salt spray and as I pulled away her eyes widened
in shock and I knew she'd read my mind.

Newspaper men

they're the trick. At Woonsocket, Rhode Island
I invited a reporter to the stationhouse
to see me escape from six sets of handcuffs.
The officers were against it at first, what with

the camera and me in a leopard-skin loincloth
like some two-bit beer hall performer.
But I freed myself in under a minute,
arms pumping like pistons to shield a pin

between my pinkie and ring finger
that I fiddled back and forth
as if I was prizing the meat from a clam,
each lock springing in turn with a satisfying click,

the cuffs coming off as easily as Bess
shimmies out of sleeves,
falling to the floor like dollar signs.
The first words of a Chinese whisper.

In Terra Pax
Paul Brownsey

Simon lets Arthur hold his hand even though he doesn't hold it as a hospital patient should, like someone merely drawing human comfort from it. He holds it in a lover's way, caressing the knuckles with his thumb, stroking it with his other hand. He even kisses it. Arthur is, of course, exploiting the circumstances to force him to endure a public show of affection. Simon notes the sly glances to check how he takes this. He calls up his resolution, all those years ago, that Arthur needed him; needed him to put up with his ways.

Actually it's all right, because the two beds opposite have been vacated since Simon's last visit and the occupant of the third seems asleep. But the hospital's pious antiseptic smell, that normally draws forth your best self, all grateful and benign, is powerless to protect Simon from the old tormenting thought: you would have left me.

Arthur's voice is for hailing someone across the street. 'DO YOU KNOW HOW I HAVE BEEN OCCUPYING MY MIND WHILE I HAVE BEEN LYING HERE AT DEATH'S DOOR?'

Has his operation somehow reduced his ability to monitor his own voice-level? But he greeted Simon normally enough when he arrived.

'I HAVE BEEN TRYING TO THINK OF THE PERFECT MASS.' A bellow on the last word. 'MADE UP OF THE BEST BITS OF THE OTHERS.'

'I'm just here.' Simon's voice has shrunk to a compensating whisper. His wiry frame that's never filled out sufficiently is helpless. 'There's no need to shout.'

'FOR THE KYRIE, I THINK IT WILL HAVE TO BE BACH, DON'T YOU? THE B MINOR MASS. NO OTHER KYRIE TRANSPORTS US SO INSISTENTLY INTO THE HEART OF THE TRANSCENDENT.' He eyes the next bed. 'WRITTEN, BY THE WAY, OR PERHAPS NOT BY THE WAY, BY A PROTESTANT.'

Another bellow on the last word. Only an archway separates this bay from a corridor patrolled by remorseless doctors and nurses on the look-out for things to reprehend. Whatever authority figure Arthur's shouting may draw, Simon resolves not to withdraw his hand from Arthur's. Yet I know you would have left me, Arthur Molyneux, even though you never did and never threatened to and the time is long past when anything could prove it one way or the other.

'THE GLORIA. HMM. NOT THE ONE IN THE CORONATION MASS, WHICH SOUNDS AS IF MOZART IS YELPING WITH DELIGHT AT THE RANGE OF FRAGRANCES ON SALE IN JOHN LEWIS'S. NOT MACMILLAN'S, EITHER: SUCH A SCREECH OF A GLORIA, LIKE HE'S DISCOVERED SOMETHING NASTY IN THE WOODSHED. WELL, POOR BOY, HE DOES THINK OF HIMSELF HARD DONE BY, AS A CATHOLIC IN THE WEST OF SCOTLAND. AS IF CATHOLICS NEVER WENT IN FOR BIGOTRY THEMSELVES.'

'Please, Arthur. Sh.'

'He is,' says Arthur, 'only pretending to sleep. IT IS IN FACT HARD TO THINK OF A GLORIA THAT DOES JUSTICE TO THE GLORY THAT IS ITS SUBJECT-MATTER. SO LET US HAVE A GLORIA THAT DOES NOT EVEN TRY TO DO SO, THAT BY ITS VERY SIMPLICITY CONVEYS GLORY ONLY IN ABSENTIA: THE GLORIA IN ARVO PÄRT'S MISSA SYLLABICA. THOUGH THE IN TERRA PAX MUST BE VIVALDI'S, OF COURSE, FROM RV 589: PEACE YEARNED FOR WITH AN ACHE TOO GREAT FOR THE SOUL TO BEAR; ALMOST.'

His eyes are on the next bed again. The man wears heavy-framed glasses as he slumbers. They and the full head of springy black hair could belong to a swotty youth eager to tell you of his discoveries about life, but the face is also doughy with disillusion and endurance.

'AND FOR THE QUI TOLLIS... SOMETHING STARK AND STERN? FOR MOST DEFINITELY, SIMON, YOU AND I HAVE SINS TO BE TAKEN AWAY, THOUGH NATURALLY THE BASTARDS INSIST THEY HATE ONLY THE SIN AND LOVE US SINNERS. AS THOUGH THERE WERE A DIFFERENCE, WHICH IN OUR CASE THERE CANNOT BE. THE PUCCINI? NO, TOO MUCH LIKE SOMETHING SUNG ON THE BARRICADES IN LES MISÉRABLES. LET'S NOT THINK ABOUT STERNNESS AND STARKNESS AND DEFIANCE. WE'LL HAVE THE QUI TOLLIS FROM HAYDN'S PAUKENMESSE. A WARM, COSSETING CELLO SOLO TAKES YOU INTO IT, AND HAVING YOUR SINS TAKEN AWAY IS LIKE EATING CHOCOLATES WITH BRANDY BY A FIRESIDE. PASS ME YOUR CHOCOLATE BOX, SIMON. '

The pyjamas on the man in the next bed: they aren't Paisley-patterned after all. The yellowish-brown blobs against a pale blue background are teddy bears.

'FOR THE DIES IRAE—FOR I DO NOT PROPOSE TO DISTINGUISH A REQUIEM MASS FROM YOUR COMMON OR GARDEN MASS, FOR EVERY MASS IS ABOUT DEATH—NOT THE VERDI, I THINK.   IT HAS THE TERROR BUT IS TOO CRUDE, TOO EARTHBOUND.'

Why is a middle-aged man wearing pyjamas in a child's pattern?

'AND MOZART'S DIES IRAE IS JUST THE WAILING SOUNDTRACK TO HELL—THE MOVIE. NO, THE DURUFLÉ, I THINK. DURUFLÉ'S DIES IRAE HAS THE TERROR, FOR WHO CAN AVOID TERROR WHEN HE THINKS OF WHAT HIS LIFE HAS BEEN?'

He gives Simon the sidelong glance combining suspicion with a knowing smirk that a quarter of a century before made it Simon's mission to seek out the real person behind the rambling pontificating about life and literature that were fuelled both by alcohol and by Arthur's conception of what his Irishness demanded of him. He takes Simon's hand to his lips again and murmurs, 'Of that terror you have been, for me, the sole assuagement. Indeed, YOU HAVE BEEN MY MASS. BUT THE DURUFLÉ DIES IRAE HAS SO MUCH MORE THAN TERROR: THE PROFOUNDEST COMPASSION. WHICH IS NOT ALWAYS DISPLAYED BY THOSE WHOSE OFFICIAL

BUSINESS IS WITH THE MASS. IS IT?'

If the chance had offered, oh how swiftly you would have dumped me and got yourself a wife. A headship: far too visible a position to be occupied by a poof living with another poof.

'DURUFLÉ'S REQUIEM HAS THE FULL DISTILLATION OF THE TERROR AND THE COMPASSION THAT ARE, BOTH OF THEM, OUR HUMAN HERITAGE. BUT LIFE THROWS THEM AT US IN SUCH JUMBLES AND DILUTIONS THAT WE NEED THE MASS TO BRING THEM TO US IN THEIR PURE, PURE FORMS, AS IN DREAMS WE FEEL THE PURE FORMS OF THE EMOTIONS, WITHOUT DISTRACTION, DILUTION OR MITIGATION.' The voice sinks. 'He's a priest, you see. And the Duruflé Requiem reminds me of something else. While I have been lying here at death's door I have been thinking back over my life. Drawing up the accounts. Staring death in the face makes you like that.'

Simon is taken over by a memory. He's a boy, in the back garden on a snowy winter's day, clutching a fire-blackened tin can that his father has made into a hand-warmer by filling it with— could it really have been embers from the garden fire?—wouldn't they be so hot that the metal would scorch you?

Suddenly it is the priest who is warming his hands on the tin can.

'You are not listening to me, Simon.' Even now that Arthur is bedridden his stocky build and boxer's brutal face confirm Simon's schoolboy immaturity.

'Sorry.'

'What the, in some lights, youthful features of Father Mahony distracted you from was this question: why was I not a professional success?' The hand that does not hold Simon's wags a finger. 'I failed to become a head teacher because of the Duruflé Requiem.'

A dramatic pause cues the general public to be startled and intrigued by the oracular remark.

'That Future Leadership in Education conference at Crieff I was summoned to after local government re-organization. Totally useless yack-yack-yack, of course, merely something to put on a CV, nothing whatsoever to do with the fire and magic of real teaching. To my certain knowledge every principal teacher who went subsequently became a head. But! I chose not to go. I knew there were, there are, things in life more important than career success. Or the salary that goes with it. And when I didn't go my card was marked. So no headship for me. I had integrity. OH YES, WE CAN BE PEOPLE OF INTEGRITY, WHATEVER SOME MAY SAY.

'You will be wondering what was more important to me than career success.' His stare invites Simon to guess.

Simon looks away and Arthur barks out a laugh. 'Choral Union that weekend, the Duruflé Requiem. FUCKED if I was going to miss singing that.'

It is, of course, perfectly natural that Arthur has been brooding on his old headship ambition simultaneously with its piercing Simon again, for they are one flesh and therefore blessed or burdened by secret visitations of the same thoughts.

'NOW AS FOR THE ET INCARNATUS EST... YOU KNOW THAT THAT IS THE HEART OF THE MASS. WHERE GOD TAKES ON HUMAN FLESH OR, AS I PREFER TO SAY, HUMAN FLESH SHINES FORTH IN ITS DIVINITY. NOT MOZART'S SOPPY ET INCARNATUS EST IN THE C MINOR MASS, LIKE SOME INSIPID MAIDEN IN PASTORAL OPERA TRILLING ON ABOUT HOW HER SHEPHERD-BOY IS TRUE. WHICH, BY THE WAY, I SUPPOSE YOU ARE NOT BEING WHILE I LIE HERE SUFFERING. Now don't get sulky and protesting. That was said solely because we have a reputation to maintain for RAMPANT PROMISCUITY.

'HAYDN AGAIN, I THINK. DON'T YOU? THE PAUKENMESSE AGAIN. GOOD OLD HAYDN, WHO KNEW THAT DIVINITY BEING MADE FLESH IS A MIRACLE, YES, BUT A QUIET, HUMANE, PATIENT ONE, TO WHICH THE ONLY APT RESPONSE IS A MELTING OF THE HEART.'

'Whereas it never melted your fucking heart that your headship ambitions would mean abandoning me,' Simon wants to say, but doesn't.

106

'FOR THE CRUCIFIXUS: SOMETHING SEARING AND AGONISED, OF COURSE. THAT IS SOMETHING WE CAN IDENTIFY WITH, SIMON, FOR WE HAVE BEEN CRUCIFIED ENOUGH AND WOULD BE STILL IF THEY HAD THEIR WAY. HE WAS DESPISÈD, AS WE ARE BY HIS NIBS. I THINK THE CRUCIFIXUS FROM MOZART'S TRINITY MASS, K 167. THOSE THUMPS IN THE ORCHESTRA: CAN'T YOU JUST FEEL THE NAILS GOING IN?'

Suddenly Simon knows why he's wearing teddy-bear pyjamas. It's a form of mortification. Prada shoes for the Pope out of the offerings of the faithful, but no designer pyjamas for this man. He knows they make him, as a priest, look ridiculous, knows they lower him from his status and dignity, and he wears them just because they do. The priest has had to set aside self entirely to become a pure channel of judgement and absolution; and of something else, too, that has even more power than the hospital smell to elevate you hygienically above your shoddiness. Yet that sublime function is exercised by a man with this ordinary, warm, sour, body and the paradox is proclaimed by his absurd choice of pyjamas. Does he have an erection when he wakes in the morning, like many men? But he could hardly proclaim that.

'AND WE'LL HAVE A LIBERA ME, THOUGH OF COURSE THERE IS ONE FORM OF LIBERATION THAT HIS KIND WOULD NEVER ALLOW. LIBERA ME. RELEASE ME. NOT THE ENGELBERT HUMPERDINCK VERSION. THE DURUFLÉ AGAIN, I THINK. THAT MAGICAL MOMENT WHEN THE GLOOMY UNGAINLY TUNE IS REPEATED AND THE HARMONY SHIFTS AND ALL WEIGHT FALLS AWAY AND YOU REALISE YOU HAVE BEEN IN PARADISE ALL ALONG...'

But there is no release from the thought that Arthur would have left him. Arthur, with his over-large head and shock of hair that's been grey since his twenties, is not a being who is necessarily there, without the possibility of absence, as God would be if he existed. This fact about Arthur hollows out the world like a blown egg and spins the world a thousand times too fast and life flies off it and the universe dies.

'AND SO WE COME TO THE OLD GLASGOW BIDDY, AGNES DAY, AND HER POSH FRIEND FROM KELVINSIDE, DONNA NOBBS. OH, THERE'S ONLY ONE POSSIBLE AGNUS DEI, ISN'T THERE? BACK TO BACH. BACK TO THE B MINOR. AN IMMENSE DRAMA HAS BEEN PLAYED OUT, THERE IS UNSPEAKABLE GRIEF AND UNSPEAKABLE COMFORT AND IT IS ALL COMPRESSED INTO THAT ALTO SOLO THAT GOES DOWN, DOWN INTO THE DEPTHS THAT, ASTONISHINGLY, ARE NOT THE DEPTHS OF HELL BUT WATERS THAT HIDE AND CLEANSE AND RESTORE. YOU HAVE PARTICIPATED IN THE GREATEST THING IN THE UNIVERSE. NO, YOU ARE THE GREATEST THING IN THE UNIVERSE.

'YOU KNOW, SIMON, SOMEONE OVERHEARING ME TALKING SO POETICALLY AND SEARCHINGLY ABOUT THE PERFECT MASS MIGHT THINK I WAS A ROMAN CATHOLIC.'

'Uh…it's not really overhearing, Arthur.'

'BUT IT IS ALL FALSE, THE MASS. EVERY WORD OF IT.' Now he looks openly at the priest. 'NO BEING BORN OF A VIRGIN AND BEING SACRIFICED FOR OUR SINS AND RISING FROM THE DEAD AND SITTING ON THE RIGHT HAND OF GOD.'

'Arthur, please stop.' Stop pulling out the priest's life-support tubes.

'OH, THERE IS TRUTH IN THE MASS BUT IT LIES A BLOODY SIGHT DEEPER THAN ANYTHING EVER DREAMT OF IN THAT WANKER'S PHILOSOPHY.'

'Arthur, stop it.'

'ON SOME LIPS IT IS PROFOUNDLY TRUE BUT ON HIS LIPS EVERY WORD IS FUCKING BOLLOCKS.'

'Arthur, if you don't stop I will leave you.'

He adds, 'I mean leave here, now. I mean it.'

But that would abandon the priest more completely to Arthur's mercy.

Without for a moment abandoning the sotto voce that propriety demands in a hospital ward, Simon blazes: 'Look. Keyhole surgery on your gall bladder is not death's door. And I'll tell you why you never got your headship. Your fucking headship. Just remember the mornings I couldn't get you out of bed because you were hungover. There were some things you were willing to sacrifice to your career, but booze wasn't one of them. And as for integrity... you told them a lie, that your mother was ill. Nothing about refusing to give up singing some requiem. Some integrity.'

There is a darkening of the light. A pale woman in black with very red lipstick meticulously applied stands in the archway leading to their wee bay of beds. Her black coat—a black fur coat, needing such courage to wear it through the grubby streets outside this hospital—is open, revealing a shiny black dress with flared skirt. There is a little black pill-box hat with a half veil. She might be on her way to some society function in the 1950s.

But Arthur is staring at Simon in prolonged appraisal. 'Oh dear.' He reaches for the spouted cup of barley water. He dribbles the liquid onto his pyjamas: his feebleness, his illness. 'Integrity,' he croaks, so softly that Simon's head is drawn very close, 'is not the same as speaking truth, and can tolerate a lie if the lie secures you from the world's unjust displeasure and penalties, and may even'—a jabbed finger undermines the show of feebleness —'demand a lie, as when the world's warfare is against the deep heart's core. It is a mark of shallow people to believe that integrity must always manifest itself in declaring truth.' His breath is lemony with barley water.

Their heads remain close as they watch her plumping up and rearranging the priest's pillows, talking softly to him. He bends forward at her behest: his face is engulfed by the fur coat and will be up against the stiff black bodice. Her movements waft across a perfume of transforming purity, nothing like incense. Notwithstanding her posh clothes she is all care. The fur coat billowing, she sweeps on her high heels to the sink in the corner, changing the water in the priest's jug, elegantly rinsing his glass. Droplets on the black fur, perhaps, but it's too far to see. There's a cheap grey plastic stacking chair at the bedside; as she tidies it away to the head of the bed her scarlet nails transmute it into an artefact of subtle avant-garde design fit for an art museum.

Arthur murmurs, 'The cardinal's mistress. Perhaps not quite all of them go after little boys. No, the cardinal in drag. Come to instruct Father Mahony—pronounced Maanee, you know, not Muh-hoe-nee—in the latest anathemas he is to issue against me and you and all our kind. Not his housekeeper, for sure. Nothing like Mrs what's-her-name in Father Ted. And not a nun, dressed like that. Mrs Doyle. And yet why not a nun? Can you be sure, these days? Lesbians have been observed wearing frocks.'

He is watching Simon's still-affronted face. He cajoles: 'May there not be an order of nuns that dresses like society women of the 1950s? Founded by Evelyn Waugh.'

Eventually Simon meets his eye. 'The Rich Clares instead of the Poor Clares.'

Now the sidelong appraising look is accompanied by a smile. 'Excellent!' cries Arthur, and they laugh together, much more than the joke warrants, and, as often when Simon is suffused by delight at Arthur's manifest approval, the thought comes to him that while Arthur got a third in English Literature, he has a Ph.D, albeit in maths. He discovers with pleasure that at no point has he withdrawn his hand from Arthur's.

'I see you can talk normally enough when I'm here. Less of the shouting, if you please.' She stands at the entrance to their bay. She's short and wide and her pale grey smock and trousers, tight across a protruding stomach, mark her out as official, though there are so many kinds of auxiliaries and specialists and administrators in hospitals these days that heaven knows what her status is. Close-cut no-nonsense grey hair, glasses enhancing large penetrating eyes.

'Sorry,' says Simon.

Her answering smile is tight and formal. She pauses in her departure to nod at the grey plastic chair at the head of the priest's bed. 'Put them in water.'

Simon has jerked to his feet, obedient like a long-limbed puppet, before he sees the spray of white lilies on the chair. The woman in black is gone.

'There's a vase down behind the sink,' Arthur says in an elaborately repentant whisper designed to placate anyone overhearing it.

Surely lilies like these, faultless as another world, breathing coolness like air-conditioning in the overheated ward, didn't come from the hospital shop. The inner trumpet is free of the stain of pollen. It doesn't matter at all that the green glass vase has a big chip out of the thick lip that protrudes 'artistically' on one side. As Simon places it on his bedside locker the priest smiles gently. 'Thank you.'

'My pleasure,' calls Arthur. 'Our pleasure. You know, I've enjoyed our talks. Perhaps when we're out of here you would come and have a meal with us. Simon cooks an excellent boeuf Bourguignonne.'

The good feeling behind Arthur's invitation: Simon rests in it absolutely; it's walled off from any scavenging doubt like some people's belief in God. Simon is reminded just how good-looking Arthur still is, in a Gordon Brownish way.

'I should like that very much,' says the priest. His voice, which seems composed of a sort of delicate outward wheeze, presumably in consequence of whatever disease laid him in this hospital bed, nevertheless contains nothing but untainted gratitude, untainted kindness. While Arthur continues, with eloquent inflections, 'Or should you be vegetarian, then I have every confidence my Simon could manage boeuf Bourguignonne without boeuf,' Simon is exultant with a question, just one: whether they will get to know the priest well enough to ask him where did he ever find an adult size in teddy-bear pyjamas.

Phil Madden

If a Frog

If a frog is found on the pavement facing the road on a mild February night after rain and a cat is skulking nearby then it is permissible and indeed admirable to offer it the option of a ride on a stick into the garden until the danger has passed.

But if the frog and the prince inside keep hopping off, this may be because of a failure to explain your honourable intentions and possibly over confident guarantees, or because they must go where the apochryphal chicken went.

Either way all you can do is wonder if this in any way helps understanding of the unfolding events in Cairo /Yemen/Libya and quietly close the door.

Quiver of the Lines

light turns
the page
what will
the swallow
bring from
Africa
is this
what pollinates
the sun
and what
when light
later closes
the book
will the
swallow take
to Africa
will it
be the
first freshness
of bluebells
or the
fading quiver
of the telegraph lines?

The Last Dodo

did the last killer sailor know that he was
did he think there were more on the rocks in the bay
did the last squalid madness know it was spent
were there not even gestures in the direction of shame

is it true that a unicorn was glimpsed in the clouds

and how was the dodo
did it scorn a blindfold
did it make a joke
did it fix the sailor with a voodoo stare

did it soliloquise
say and so it will be
for each one of you
and the insects will neither
remember nor care

just don't tell me
it simply died

just don't tell me
it simply died

Cara Watson

Birth Day

She turns,
gathers the baby
still wet, still wrinkled.

The clatter of 1927
slips through the open window.
Bitter air

clutters the halls
where babies come
and go.

Between the lines of cots
stories begin.

Photo

There you are
on the church steps
in a black and white world.

He stares from the edge,
frayed in his suit and
dead carnation.

She clutches fuchsias
that bleed into the folds
of her cold white dress.

Disappearing Act

He folded his words
into silence
went to bed
in crumpled sheets.

Sometimes he cut his wages
into flakes or
scattered fragments
of her Bible.

The final trick was to
turn himself
into Jesus
on Richmond Green.

He forgot
the magic word
as he dwindled
in a haze of blue lights.

Demolition

Dislodging the soft moss
she ripped grey slates
from the ribcage of rafters.

She told me
not to talk about rain.

The windows gave in easily,
splintered frames that lost their grip
on cracked glass.

Asylum Seeker

He spits
words
like lemon pips,

grabs apples
from
empty air.

Outside
grey geese
come honking

Contributors

Deb Baker is a writer, insatiable reader, and reference librarian. Author of *The Nocturnal Librarian* and *bookconscious*, her poems have appeared in journals and anthologies in Europe, North America, and Japan.

Elizabeth Briggs has an M.A. in Teaching and Practice of Creative Writing from Cardiff University, and is currently doing her Ph.D. at Aberystwyth University whilst writing her second novel. When she's not penning poems at midnight, she's designing creative writing lessons for adult learning courses.

Paul Brownsey has been a journalist on a local newspaper in Luton and a philosophy lecturer at Glasgow University. He lives in Bearsden. He has published about fifty short stories, most recently the winning story in the Jane Austen Short Story Award 2011, published in Wooing Mr Wickham, edited by Michèle Roberts (Honno Press).

Jacqueline Bulman has published in several magazines including *Acumen*, *New Writer* and *Other Poetry*, and in two other Cinnamon Press anthologies. She was short-listed for Bridport Prize 2010 and lives in a remote converted chapel. She mostly writes about people and how we deal with being human. She has just finished her first collection.

Joanna Campbell writes short stories all day at home in the Cotswolds, with three cats and occasional bowls of cereal for company. She has been published in various magazines and anthologies. In 2010, she was shortlisted for the Fish, Bristol and Bridport Short Story Prizes.

Catherine Coldstream was born in London and educated in the West Country and at Oxford, where she studied theology. She is a keen viola player, singer and composer, has worked in music publishing, and spent twelve years as a nun in an enclosed contemplative community. She now lives in Oxford, where she writes, performs, and teaches.

Tricia Durdey lives in Derbyshire with her husband, son, and a retired racing greyhound. She dances, writes, and teaches Pilates. She is studying for an MA in Writing at Sheffield Hallam University.

Lucy Durneen was born in Cambridge in 1978 and now lives in Cornwall. She has published short stories in *The Manchester Review* and *The Lightship Anthology 1* and has been shortlisted in a number of national and international competitions. She currently lectures in English and Creative Writing at the University of Plymouth.

Rosie Garland has an eclectic writing and performance history, from 80s Goth band *The March Violets*, to twisted cabaret as alter ego *Rosie Lugosi the Vampire Queen*. With widely anthologised poetry, short stories and essays, she's also won the DaDa Award for Performance Artist of the Year and the Diva Award for Solo Performer.

Ken Head is presently based in England, although for many years he lived in South-East Asia. His work appears regularly in print and online publications. To date, he has published one full poetry collection, *Listening For Light* and three chapbooks, *Long Shadows, A Devil's Dozen* and *Still Lives*. His website is www.kenhead.co.uk.

Jo Hemmant lives with her family in rural Kent. Her poems have appeared in various magazines and anthologies and she has won prizes in competitions. Last year she decided to combine her many years of experience in publishing with her love of poetry and set up Pindrop Press.

Anne Hine Anne Hine has lived in the North-East for the last thirty years. She began writing seriously in the 1990's and her first poetry pamphlet *Dark Matters* was published by Vane Women Press in 2001. She is presently working towards a further collection and has had work published in several anthologies.

Lindsey Holland's poetry and reviews have appeared in publications including *Tears in the Fence, Ink, Sweat & Tears* and *The Oxfam Anthology of Young British Poets*. Her pamphlet *Particle Soup* will be published this year. She is Poetry Editor for *Sabotage Reviews* and is the founder member of North West Poets. She blogs at http://particlesoup.blogspot.com.

Janet Holst is a New Zealander currently living in Oman. She has taught in Melanesia, New Zealand, South Africa and the Middle East. Her stories have been published in South Africa and Australia, and academic articles in various journals.

Alex Josephy lives in the East End of London and works in the NHS as an education adviser. He has had poems published in *The Rialto*, *Smiths Knoll*, *The Interpreter's House* and others. In 2010 He won a second prize in the Hippocrates competition, and was placed in the Troubadour top twenty.

Amy Mackelden is a writer and teacher from the Isle of Wight, and is now based in Gateshead. In 2011 she won a Northern Promise Award for poetry from New Writing North. She is half of microfiction and music duo The Copy Room, with banjoist Dan Walsh (www.copyroom.co.uk).

Phil Madden will never get over the sending off in the Rugby World Cup. Poems of loss are certain. Slightly less seriously, he is collaborating with various visual artists-and would now like to add a joint venture on Japanese tea ceremonies. Anyone interested?

Ian McEwen studied philosophy and then worked in investment banking before returning to writing in 2002. His poems have appeared in *Smiths Knoll*, *Poetry Wales* and *Poetry Review* among others. He is on the board of *Magma*.   His pamphlet *The Stammering Man* was a winner in the Templar competition 2010.

Jane McLaughlin poems have been widely published in magazines and anthologies, including several Cinnamon Press publications. She won the Cinnamon Press Writing Award in November 2010 for her story *A Roof of Red Tiles*. She lives in London and works as a freelance in further education and academic publishing.

Eithne Nightingale works as Head of Diversity and Equality at the V&A Museum and has published extensively on the arts and diversity. She has also had publications of travel, fiction and memoir writing in the UK and Australia and has won or been runner up in writing competitions. She is a keen photographer. For more of her work visit: www.eithnenightingale.com.

David Olsen second poetry chapbook, *New World Elegies*, is new from Finishing Line Press. His work has been published in dozens of British and American journals; since 2008 his poems have appeared in *Envoi, Acumen, Orbis, Assent, The Interpreter's House, Poetry Nottingham, Oxford Magazine, Writing Magazine* and competition anthologies.

Ben Parker completed a creative writing MA at UEA in 2008. His work has appeared in a number of magazines, including *Staple, Ink Sweat & Tears, Iota* and *Neon*.

Aisling Tempany has appeared in four previous Cinnamon Press anthologies since 2009, as well as recently appearing in the Templar Press anthology *Bliss*. She lives in Wales, and is studying part-time as a postgraduate in Swansea University, writing on Irish Modernists.

Nicola Warwick was born in Kent and lives in Suffolk. She has had poems in magazines including The Rialto, Iota and South, as well as in previous Cinnamon Press anthologies.

Cara Watson was born in 1960. She left school with few qualifications but subsequently gained a BA and MA in English Literature. She has been writing poetry seriously for about 5 years and been helped by the Open University Creative writing Diploma course and Bill Greenwell's Poetry Online Workshops. She has two children and a large family of animals plus a very supportive husband.

Noel Williams is widely published in anthologies and magazines, including *Iota, Envoi, The North* and *Wasafiri* and has won many prizes. He has an MA in creative writing from Sheffield Hallam University where he's also a lecturer. He's co-editor of *Antiphon* magazine (antiphon.org.uk) and reviews editor for *Orbis*. Website: http://noelwilliams.wordpress.com/

Martin Willitts, Jr. recent poetry chapbooks include *True Simplicity* (Poets Wear Prada Press, 2011), *Why Women Are A Ribbon Around A Bomb* (Last Automat, 2011), *Art Is Always an Impression of What an Artist Sees* (Muse Café, 2011), and *Secrets No One Wants To Talk About* (Dos Madres Press, 2011).

Margaret Wilmot studied at the University of California in Berkeley before taking jobs in Italy and Greece. She has lived in Sussex since 1978. Sources of interest and inspiration keep expanding and changing but at present include the connections based on memory, natural history, painting, science, life.